All About the Human Body

ALL
ABOUT

the
Human
Body

by Bernard Glemser

Illustrated by
Felix Traugott

RANDOM
HOUSE
NEW YORK

allabout
books

To ROBERT MARTIN STEINMAN

for his help with this and other projects

Contents

The Secret Life of Your Body

Nothing in the world is so wonderful as the human body. The more we discover about it, the more wonderful and exciting it seems.

But nearly everything your body does is hidden from sight, and as a result you are hardly ever aware of what is going on. You cannot see your heart beating, for example. You cannot see how your lungs function, or how your food is digested, or how your muscles enable you to move. All this happens secretly inside you.

There is one time, though, when you can really see your body at work. That is when you cut yourself. Now and then we all get little cuts and scratches which do us no great harm. But even the smallest cut brings the secret forces of your body into action. Then you can see how efficiently your body looks after you.

You know what happens if, by accident, you cut your finger slightly. First, you feel a twinge of pain, and you snatch your finger away from whatever cut you. A little blood flows out. Then, quite soon, the blood stops flowing and gradually a red skin or scab forms over the cut. In a few days this scab grows smaller and disappears. Only a small white scar is left to remind you of your accident, and usually this, too, vanishes within a short time.

Have you ever wondered what really happens to that little cut? If you think about it, there are all sorts of questions which need to be answered. Why did it hurt when you cut yourself? Why did the blood stop flowing out of the cut after a few minutes? How did the cut turn into a scar? What is a scar made of? And how did new skin grow over the scar?

First of all, the twinge of pain was really a warning from your brain. Your brain is the control center of your body. An important part of its work is to protect you from injury. But occasionally it cannot prevent a little slip, and the pain you feel is an urgent message saying, "Look out, there! Be more careful!" So at once you snatch your finger out of harm's way.

Possibly, just for a moment, you were frightened

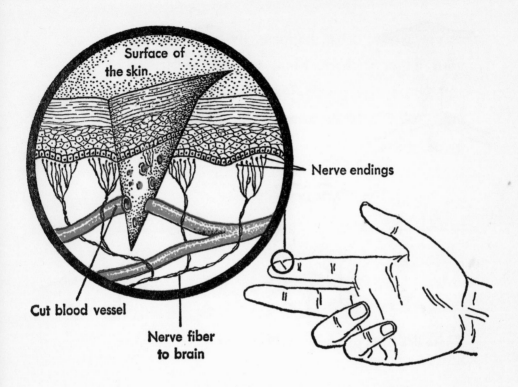

Surface of
the skin

Nerve endings

Cut blood vessel

Nerve fiber
to brain

A cut in the skin as seen through a microscope.

when you saw that your finger was bleeding. Fortunately, losing a little blood is not very serious because your body has plenty in reserve, and it also makes new blood quite quickly. But losing a great deal of blood might be serious, and this could happen if the cut remained open for a long time. For this reason, the cut has to be closed and sealed as quickly as possible.

There is another reason, just as important, why the cut must be sealed. Tiny microbes or bacteria, so small

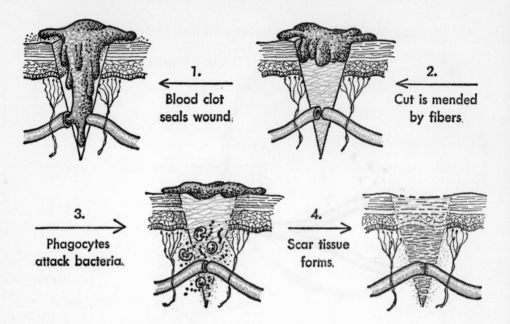

1.

← **Blood clot seals wound.**

2.

← **Cut is mended by fibers.**

3.

→ **Phagocytes attack bacteria.**

4.

→ **Scar tissue forms.**

These drawings of a small cut show steps in the healing process.

that you cannot even see them with a powerful magnifying glass, might enter the cut and cause an infection. This could be dangerous, particularly if you do not take care of it.

Therefore, your body immediately goes to work to safeguard you from harm. Its first task is to close the cut; and it does this by causing the blood to clot. What happens is that the drops of blood coming out of the cut begin to thicken. They cling together. Instead of being liquid, the blood turns to a sort of jelly that fills the cut completely. Before long, this jelly hardens, forming a seal which prevents blood from leaking out and also prevents bacteria from creeping in.

This seal is only the first step toward closing the wound. It could easily be broken again. So, gradually, it is made harder and stronger, while your body begins the complicated work of building new skin. Finally it becomes a small red scab.

But dangerous bacteria might have entered the cut at the time the accident happened or while the scab was being formed, and it is important that these should be destroyed before they can cause any serious harm. This is the task of special cells in your body called phagocytes, which means "eating cells." They are part of your body's defense against disease. When they encounter any dangerous microbe in your body, they destroy it by wrapping themselves around it and engulfing it.

Meanwhile, your body is closing and repairing the cut. It uses the red scab as the framework or scaffolding for its work, drawing the edges of the cut together, clearing away the debris of the damaged skin, closing the gap with strong fibers. Only when the cut has been filled in completely is the scab ready to fall off. What you see then is scar tissue. It is not really skin, which is softer and more elastic and consists of several distinct layers. Scar tissue is tough, not very elastic, and much whiter than skin. That is why a scar is so noticeable. But it is a permanent seal—in fact, it is even stronger than the skin itself. Also, it has a special quality of contracting, which means that gradually it grows smaller and smaller, drawing the edges of the cut more tightly together.

Finally, new skin begins to grow over the scar tissue. It may take some time, but when this process is complete you will find it hard to see where the little cut was originally. Your body will have repaired itself almost perfectly. The cut, the scab, the scar—all will have gone. And this is a simple example of the quiet and efficient way in which your body works, day after day, taking care of you.

But where does the new skin come from? How does it grow?

For that matter, how does any part of your body grow? How did you grow from a tiny baby, weighing just a few pounds when you were born, to the size you now are?

The answers are part of the dramatic story of how your body grows.

How Your
Body Grows

Until recently nobody knew how any living thing
grows. It was a mystery which even the most learned
doctors could not explain. It almost seemed as if a
blade of grass, or a kitten, or a baby, just stretched a
little more every day until it was fully grown.

Then, only about a hundred and twenty years ago,
an astounding discovery was made. Two German scientists named Schleiden and Schwann helped to prove
that all living things are built of tiny units called cells,
much as a wall is built of units called bricks. This was
probably the most important discovery in biology, the
science of life. It helped to explain many mysteries
about the human body. In particular, it helped to explain how we grow, and how new skin grows over
a cut.

All About the Human Body

Your entire body is built of cells. There are about thirty thousand million million of them; and of course they are all incredibly tiny. For example, your blood contains an enormous number of red cells, which give blood its red color. Although these are among the largest cells in the body, each one is only about 1/3000 of an inch in diameter.

You can only see what a cell is like by using a microscope, which is an instrument for making tiny objects look larger. Scientists now have very powerful microscopes which enable them to examine in detail the smallest of cells. Also, they have wonderful machines called micro-manipulators which are fitted with very fine needles. With one of these machines attached to a microscope, a cell can actually be taken apart. In this way scientists learn more about the way it is made.

Suppose, then, that you are in a modern laboratory, and that you are looking at a single cell under a very powerful microscope equipped with a micro-manipulator.

Human cells are found in many different shapes; the one you have chosen to examine is almost circular.

You can see at once that it has a sort of skin around it. This is called the membrane. If you touch it gently

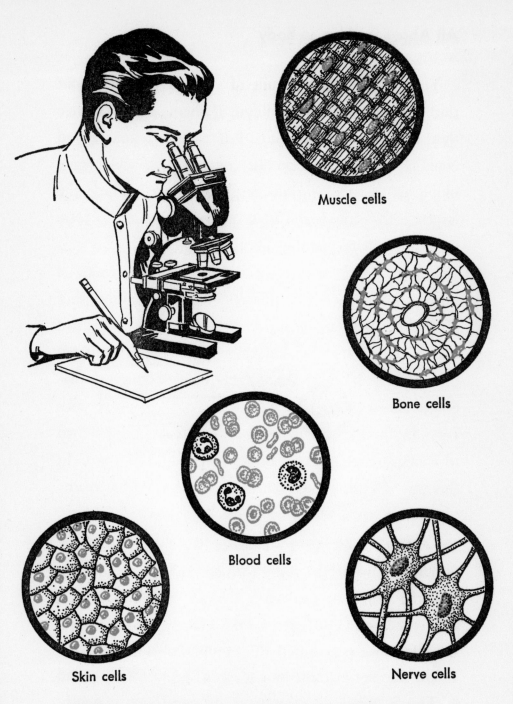

Muscle cells

Bone cells

Blood cells

Skin cells

Nerve cells

In the microscope we can see the shape of different cells.

with one of the tiny needles of the micro-manipulator, you will find that the membrane can be pressed in easily. When you remove the needle, the cell resumes its shape. This means that the cell can squeeze itself into almost any position. The membrane is also porous in a special way, so that chemicals which the cell needs can seep in, and waste products, which the cell does not need, can seep out.

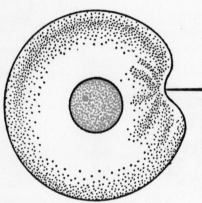

Cell membrane
pressed in
by microneedle.

Cells are made of a substance we call protoplasm, which means the first thing formed. When you look inside the cell, you can see a whitish substance with a darker center. This part of the cell protoplasm has a special name: it is called the cytoplasm, which simply means the material out of which the body of the cell is formed. It is actually a soft watery jelly. Your needle can go right into it without disturbing it too much.

Now you can explore the darker mass in the center of the cell. This is called the nucleus, and it holds the great and fascinating mystery of life.

The nucleus controls the cell. If you remove the nucleus, the cell cannot reproduce itself, and eventually it will die. If you cut the cell in two unequal parts, the part containing the nucleus can repair itself and go on living normally.

If you look closely inside the nucleus of a cell which is getting ready to divide, you will see the most mysterious particles of our bodies, a tangle of tiny threadlike objects called the chromosomes. There are actually 48 of them, and this number is the same for all human beings. Other species have different numbers. For example, the cells of dogs have 52 chromosomes each, those of horses have 60. And in some way that scientists do not yet understand, the chromosomes carry even smaller particles called the genes. From the time your life begins, the genes seem to control your growth and to some extent your personality. They decide what you will inherit from your father and mother, the color of your eyes and your hair, and so on.

All the cells in your body came from one special kind

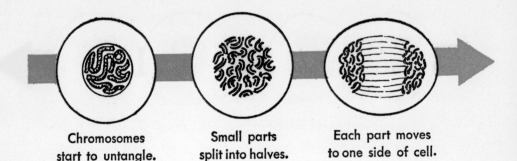

Chromosomes
start to untangle.

Small parts
split into halves.

Each part moves
to one side of cell.

of cell which is called the ovum, or egg cell. This is the female cell, and it has only 24 chromosomes, which is half the usual number. Therefore, it is not really complete. It only becomes complete when it unites with a male cell, which also has 24 chromosomes, so that altogether there are 48. All the cells in your body are descended from this completed or fertilized cell.

The way in which our cells multiply is fascinating. The cell grows slightly in size. Then changes appear within the nucleus and the membrane of the nucleus disappears. Each of the chromosomes divides into two parts, making twice the usual number. There are now 96 chromosomes. These separate and form two groups of 48 chromosomes, each group going to opposite sides of the cell. Finally, the cell—which has stretched into a shape rather like a dumbbell—breaks apart into two equal parts, each with its own nucleus containing 48

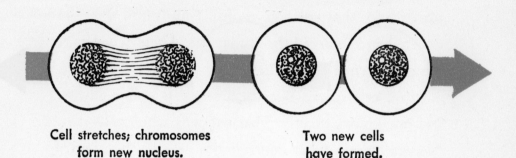

Cell stretches; chromosomes
form new nucleus.

Two new cells
have formed.

chromosomes. Now there are two cells where there was only one before.

But the body needs cells of several different kinds. Almost as soon as there are a few dozen cells, they begin to change slightly, preparing for the special work they do when your body is fully formed. Groups of the same kind of cells weave themselves together to form the tissues of the body. Some form the skin; others the muscles, the bones, the nerves, and the strong tissue that connects and supports the organs of the body. The organs, such as the heart and the stomach, consist of several kinds of tissue.

But the units from which tissues and organs are built are cells. They are the building blocks of the body.

You can now understand what happens in the last stages of healing a cut on your finger. The skin cells around the edges of the cut multiply more rapidly than usual; and they go on multiplying until they have covered and replaced the scar tissue. Then, when everything is normal again, they stop.

How cells carry out their work is still a mystery. No one knows exactly what happens when cells divide. No one knows what controls the cells in the construction of the body. All over the world, scientists are trying to find the answers to these problems.

Why You Eat, Why You Drink and Why You Breathe

3

Have you ever wondered why you have to eat and drink so many times every day?

The simplest answer is that your body needs food and water.

Food is vital to us. We have to eat because food keeps us strong and active. Yet people have been known to live without food for several weeks.

Water is even more important to us. Without it, nobody can live for more than a few days.

And even more important to our bodies than food and water is the air around us. We cannot live for more than a few minutes without breathing.

Let us look more closely at these three processes.

All About the Human Body

We usually breathe from sixteen to twenty times each minute. If you analyzed the air you breathe, you would find it is a mixture of different gases. Most of it is nitrogen—about four-fifths. One-fifth is oxygen. There is also a tiny amount of carbon dioxide, a little water vapor (which gives air its humidity) and some traces of what are called rare gases.

If you were to put a bag over your nose and mouth to catch the air you breathe out, and then analyze this air, you would find some strange changes. There would still be the same amount of nitrogen. There would also be the same traces of rare gases. But there would be much less oxygen, and there would be a hundred times more carbon dioxide than you breathed in. There would also be considerably more water vapor.

What happens is that each time you breathe, an exchange takes place. You keep some oxygen; you breathe out very much more carbon dioxide and water vapor than you breathed in.

The reason is that every moment of the day and night your body is using up energy. Your heart uses up energy as it beats. Your muscles use up energy. So does your brain, and so does every other part of you. All this energy is produced by the work of the millions and millions of cells which make up your body. Every one of these cells needs oxygen in order to do its work.

But as the cells use up oxygen they form carbon dioxide. This is a waste product, just as smoke and ashes are the waste products of a fire. The cells must get rid of this waste as quickly as possible.

Therefore, your body carries out these two processes at the same time. You breathe in the oxygen which the cells need to produce energy, and you breathe out the carbon dioxide which is harmful. It sounds so simple. Yet your life depends on its happening day and night without interruption. There is even a special part of your brain which forces you to breathe if you try to hold your breath too long.

But why do you breathe out more water vapor than you breathe in? You can actually see it if you breathe onto a mirror. A mist forms, composed of tiny droplets of water which have been carried by your breath.

This water vapor helps to control the temperature of your body. Some of the energy being produced inside you is in the form of heat; but this heat must be controlled carefully so that your body remains at a temperature of about 98.6° Fahrenheit. If your temperature rises more than two or three degrees, it usually means that you have a fever, and you begin to feel sick and weak.

When water evaporates it carries heat away with it. This is how the water vapor which you breathe out helps to cool your body. You are cooled in the same way by sweating, which causes water to evaporate from your skin. Dogs and cats can only sweat through the pads on their paws, so they help to cool themselves by breathing rapidly. That is why they need to drink so much water in hot weather, and why they go around with their mouths open, panting.

In the course of a day you lose about a pint of water in the air you breathe out, and nearly the same amount by sweating. You also lose water in your urine and in your solid wastes. Altogether the water loss is quite considerable.

Water is essential to life for many reasons. The soft watery jelly inside your cells contains as much as sixty to ninety-nine per cent of water. More than ninety per cent of the liquid part of your blood is water. So, in one way or another, water makes up a large part of your body. If you lose more water than you drink, the entire balance of your body can be upset. If you go without water for too long, the cells themselves shrink, your blood is affected, and the temperature of your body rises.

Just as the cells and tissues of our bodies are composed largely of water, so are most of the different kinds of food we eat, such as fresh fruit and vegetables, and milk products like cheese, butter and ice cream. Food, then, provides us with some of the water we need.

But our food is important to us for other reasons. The first reason is that it supplies the fuel for all our energy.

You know that an automobile cannot run unless the motor is supplied with gasoline (which is a special kind of fuel) and also with air. The burning of the gasoline when it combines with the oxygen in the air releases energy. This drives the pistons of the motor up and down and causes the wheels of the car to turn.

Almost the same process, but much slower, takes place in the cells of our bodies. The fuel, which comes from our food, is burned by combining with the oxygen we breathe in from the air. This energy is used to do all the work the body requires.

There are three basic foods from which we get energy: fats, sugars and starches. These last two are called carbohydrates, which simply means substances formed from carbon and water. Some of the foods which provide carbohydrates are vegetables and fruits, bread, oatmeal, corn meal, rice and milk.

Fats, which we get from butter, cream and the fatty parts of meat, can be stored in the body and used when necessary.

In addition to supplying fuel for energy, food provides the materials for building our bodies. The cells require a constant supply of many different chemicals from which new cells can be built. The substances in our food which enable us to grow are called proteins. These we get from meat, fish and eggs, as well as from nuts, beans and peas.

Just as important, our food provides us with minerals which contain calcium, phosphorus and iron, without which we could not live; and it also contains the vitamins which keep us healthy.

But the food we swallow cannot go directly to our cells. Before it can be absorbed by the cells, it must be broken down into tiny particles. And the substances we need must be separated from the substances we don't need.

This is the work of the digestive system.

What Happens
When You Eat

4

Before we see what happens when you eat, let me explain how the inside of your body is arranged. It looks complicated in drawings and photographs, but it is really quite simple to understand.

Right across your body, roughly following the arch of your lower ribs, is a sheet of strong muscle called the diaphragm. It is a sort of fence dividing your body into two parts; and this, in fact, is what the name diaphragm means. The upper part is called the chest cavity, and it contains principally the heart and the lungs. The lower part is called the abdominal cavity, and this contains the organs which make up your digestive system. It contains also certain of the sexual organs, and the organs which enable you to eliminate the waste products of your food.

Even before you begin to eat, a strange thing happens.

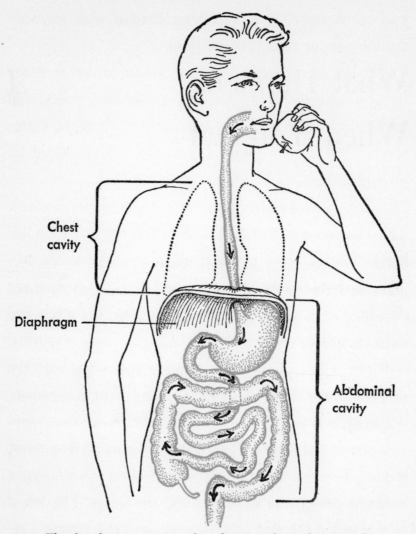

Chest cavity

Diaphragm

Abdominal cavity

The food you eat travels a long and winding road.

Your mouth starts to water. The sight of food, and particularly the smell of food, will cause it to happen. If you are hungry, it will happen even if you are only thinking about your favorite food.

The water, or saliva, in your mouth makes it easier for you to swallow. If your mouth were dry, you would find it difficult to swallow your food. The saliva, therefore, prepares your mouth for eating. It is produced by three glands on each side of your face.

Saliva does still more. As soon as you begin to eat, it starts the process of digestion. You can test this by holding a piece of bread in your mouth. Within a few seconds the bread becomes soft. There are two reasons for this. First, the water in your saliva helps to soften and dissolve the bread. Second, saliva contains a special chemical substance, called an enzyme, which acts on the starch in your food and breaks it down. There are many different kinds of enzymes. This one is called ptyalin.

It isn't enough merely to let your food become moist in your mouth. You chew it and grind it between your teeth, breaking it into small fragments. Then, when it is thoroughly chewed and moistened, your tongue carries it to the back of the mouth where it can be swallowed.

Here, something very interesting happens.

There are several openings at the back of your mouth.

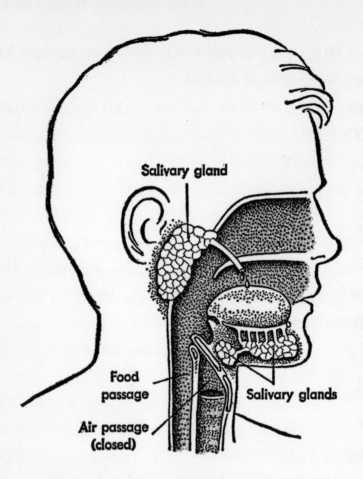

Salivary gland

Food passage

Air passage (closed)

Salivary glands

When you swallow, the air passage closes.

Two lead up into your nose; one leads down to your lungs; one leads down to your stomach. Obviously, your food must go down the right opening; so, each time you swallow, the other openings are blocked off completely. Sometimes—if you are eating in too great a hurry, or trying to talk at the same time that you are trying to eat—a little food or liquid enters the wrong passage. You cough or splutter as a result.

Connecting the back of your mouth and your stomach is a tube called the esophagus. This name comes from two Greek words, meaning *I carry what is eaten*. It is simply a passageway, lined with muscles which draw your food down smoothly. In an adult it is about nine inches long.

The stomach lies just below the diaphragm. It is shaped rather like a big pear held upside down. The esophagus enters at the side near the top.

The walls of the stomach are built of strong muscle, lined inside with about thirty-five million glands which manufacture a mixture of chemicals called gastric juice. The most important parts of gastric juice are hydrochloric acid and an enzyme called pepsin. These have a very powerful dissolving action.

The task of the stomach is to digest, or break down into tiny particles, the food you have eaten, particularly the proteins. The strong muscles of the walls of the stomach work with tremendous vigor. They tighten around the food, push it, squeeze it, roll it from side to side, mixing it with the gastric juices. This goes on for about four hours, until the food is completely soft and

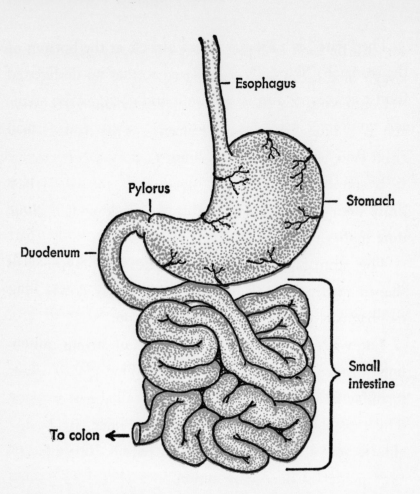

Esophagus

Pylorus

Stomach

Duodenum

Small
intestine

To colon ←

**The stomach prepares the food for digestion; the small
intestine filters it for absorption.**

almost liquid. The muscles move with a wavy motion.
They gradually sweep the semi-liquid mass down toward the narrow end of the stomach, which is called the
pylorus. This name also comes from two Greek words,
meaning *the guardian of the gate.*

The "gate" is a special round muscle at the bottom of the stomach. Normally it is closed so that no undigested food can escape. But every now and then, as the stomach completes its work, this muscle opens and a small portion of food is allowed through.

But still more must happen to your food before it is ready to be absorbed by the cells and tissues of your body. From the pylorus, the food passes into another part of your digestive tract: the small intestine. This is small only in diameter. Actually it is about twenty feet long in an adult. To fit into your body it is arranged in a tight coil, folded backward and forward several times.

The first part of the small intestine is called the duodenum, which means *twelve fingers' breadth* because this is how the old anatomists measured its length.

Meeting in the wall of the duodenum are ducts, or small tubes, from two important organs. One comes from the gall bladder, a small sac attached to your liver. This carries a substance called bile, which helps to digest fats.

The other comes from a large gland called the pancreas, lying close to the duodenum. It carries a mixture of substances called the pancreatic juice. The bile and the pancreatic juice continue the work of digestion.

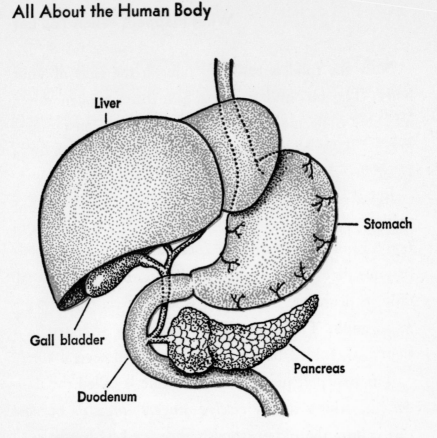

Liver

Stomach

Gall bladder

Pancreas

Duodenum

Bile from the liver is concentrated in the gall bladder and added to the food together with pancreatic juice.

They also neutralize, or stop the action of, the hydrochloric acid which was mixed with the food in your stomach.

In the duodenum, therefore, your food is digested still more thoroughly. And, as the liquid mass passes through the coils of the small intestine, digestion is completed.

Now the food is ready to nourish the cells of your body. The fats and proteins have been broken down into tiny molecules. The carbohydrates, which produce energy, have been broken down into molecules of a special form of sugar called glucose.

But these molecules cannot simply stay in the coils of the small intestine. Somehow, they must be absorbed into your body.

This is done by a marvelous process.

The inner surface of the small intestine is covered by millions of tiny tubes called villi, which means hairs, al-

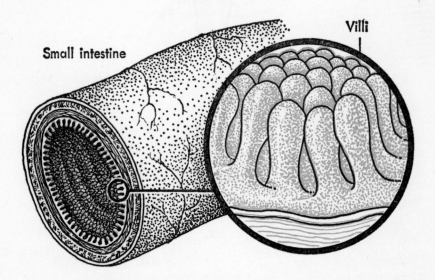

At the right is an enlargement of the villi which cover the inner surface of the small intestine.

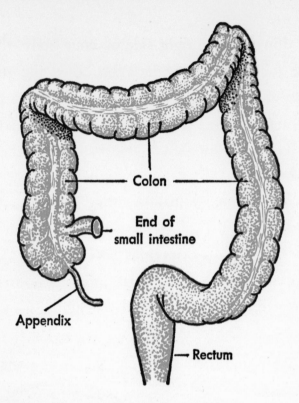

In an adult the colon is about five feet long.

though they are not really hairs. They are like tentacles, or fingers. As the digested food passes them, they move backward and forward, and up and down, sucking up the molecules of protein and glucose. Other tiny ducts suck up the molecules of fat. And, as the food travels through the coils of the small intestine, everything that will provide you with nourishment is absorbed. The rest is waste which must be expelled.

Low down on the right side of your body, the small intestine joins a much wider tube called the colon, or large intestine. The appendix, which is like a small finger, is situated here. It serves no purpose as far as we know, and it occasionally causes trouble by becoming inflamed.

The colon is about five feet long and shaped rather like three sides of a square. It goes up your right side. Then it bends sharply across your body, below your stomach. Then it bends again, coming down your left side. The end of the colon is called the rectum; this is about six inches long and follows the curve at the bottom of your spine. The rectum ends in the anal canal, which is normally kept closed by a strong circular muscle called the anal sphincter.

When the waste food products reach the colon, they are still semi-liquid after being digested. But your body cannot afford to lose so much water each time you eat. So, as the waste travels through the colon most of the water is re-absorbed. Then the waste is ready to be discharged through the anal canal.

From beginning to end, the food you eat takes about twenty-four hours to travel through your digestive system. The muscles of your stomach and intestinal tract have to work very hard indeed, particularly in the first stages of digestion. That is one reason why you often feel sleepy after a big meal.

How Your Body
Is Nourished

5

Once food has been digested and picked up by the millions of villi lining the small intestine, it is ready to be carried all over your body. Every living cell must be supplied with the food it needs, as well as water and oxygen.

These vital substances are carried by your blood through a vast network of blood vessels. Some of these blood vessels are nearly an inch in diameter. Most are so tiny that you cannot see them without a microscope. The total length of the blood vessels in the body of an adult human being is more than 12,000 miles.

Not only does your blood carry food, water and oxygen to the cells. It carries away the carbon dioxide waste which the cells do not need. In your blood, also, are millions and millions of those eating cells, or phago-cytes, which help to guard you from infection.

One of the ways in which scientists study blood is by using a machine called a centrifuge. In its simplest form this consists of a small electric motor and an ex-tension arm. One end of the arm is attached to the shaft of the motor. A test tube containing a little blood is clamped to the other end. When the motor is started, the test tube is whirled around at the rate of about 3,000 times a minute. As a result of this whirling action, the

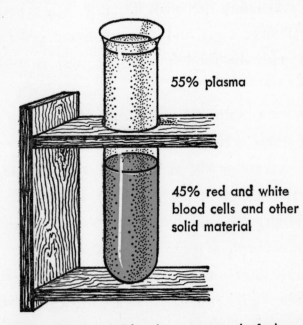

55% plasma

45% red and white blood cells and other solid material

Over half of your blood is composed of plasma.

heavier parts of the blood are thrown to the bottom of the test tube.

If you watch this experiment, you would see that within a few moments the blood separates into two distinctly different parts. A little more than half, at the top, is a clear straw-colored liquid. The part at the bottom is much thicker and red.

The clear liquid can be poured into another test tube. Now we are left with the substance which gives blood its red color.

Examined under a microscope, this red substance is very interesting.

It is composed of several kinds of cells. The most numerous are those which are actually red in color—the red cells. There are about seventy-five billion of these in a cubic inch of blood. They are shaped like little wheels with bulging rubber tires, and they tend to cling together in little heaps rather like sticky pennies which have toppled over. Unlike other cells, a red cell has no nucleus. Also it is so flexible that it can bend almost double.

Scattered among the red blood cells are other cells which are more difficult to see because they are almost

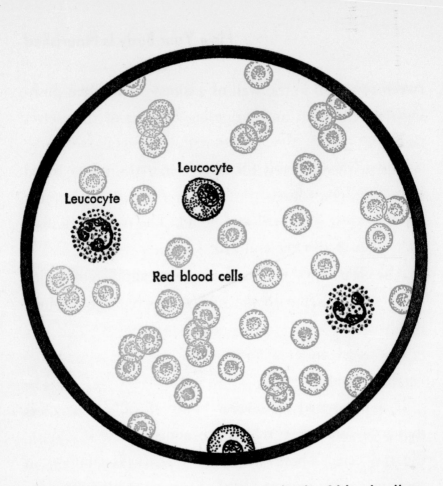

In a microscope you can see different kinds of blood cells.

transparent. These are called white cells, or leucocytes. There are about a hundred million of them in a cubic inch of blood.

Certain of these white cells are the phagocytes, or cell eaters, in your blood stream. They can even escape from blood vessels to search for enemy bacteria. They do this by squeezing a small portion of themselves between two cells in the wall of a blood vessel, then pushing the cells apart and wriggling the rest of themselves through.

But neither the red blood cells nor the white blood cells carry the digested food particles. The red cells carry oxygen all over the body and carry carbon dioxide away. The white cells protect us from infection.

Food is carried in the liquid part of the blood, called the plasma. This is the clear straw-colored liquid which rises to the top of the test tube when it is whirled in a centrifuge.

More than ninety per cent of plasma is water. The other ten per cent contains so many chemical substances that a list of them would fill several pages of this book. Plasma contains the food which you digested, except for those parts which your body has stored.

It contains carbohydrates, in the form of a sugar called glucose, which the cells use to produce energy.

It contains proteins, which have been broken down still further into substances called amino acids. Using these, your cells can build the very special proteins they need. Plasma contains more than twenty different amino acids.

It also contains its own special blood proteins which

are used by the blood in clotting when you cut yourself, and which also keep the blood thick, or viscous. It contains sodium, potassium, calcium, magnesium, iodine and iron, in many chemical forms. It carries the hormones which look after your growth and control the activity of the organs of your body.

And it also contains mysterious substances called antibodies which guard your health. Antibodies are not living cells, like phagocytes; they are chemicals which some tissues produce to destroy dangerous bacteria.

We still have to see how your food gets into the blood stream from the tiny villi in the small intestine.

Each of the millions of villi has its own tiny, complete blood system. Each has a blood vessel called an artery, which brings blood in; and a blood vessel called a vein, which carries blood away from it.

As your food is digested, the villi pick up the food particles and pass them into the veins. These veins join larger and larger veins, like the branches of a tree. At last they reach a very large vein which is like one of the biggest branches of the tree. This is called the portal vein, and it carries all the particles of digested food—except most of the fats—to the liver.

The liver is the largest organ in your body. In an

adult it weighs a little more than three pounds. It is shaped rather like a wedge and lies under the diaphragm, mostly on the right side of the body. It is protected there by the lower ribs. The pointed part reaches more than halfway across your body, above the stomach.

Scientists are still trying to understand how the liver does all its work. They have discovered that it does more

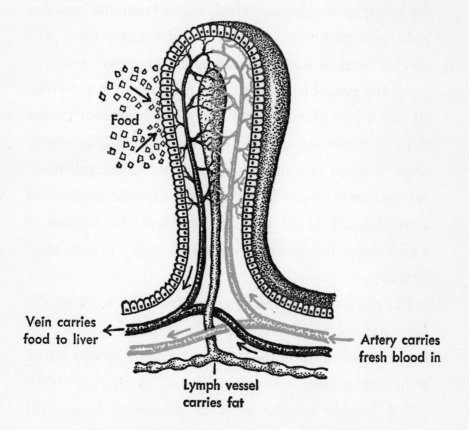

Food

Vein carries
food to liver

Artery carries
fresh blood in

Lymph vessel
carries fat

An enlargement of villi of the small intestine

than seventy different things, but how it works is still unknown. Inside, the liver consists simply of groups of cells called lobules. Blood circulates through each lobule until it reaches a vein in the center. All these central veins join again into larger veins which carry the blood to the heart.

The liver is like an intricate chemical factory. It takes the particles of glucose which came from the starches and sugars you ate and digested and changes them into another kind of carbohydrate called glycogen which it stores for you. Then, when you need sugar, it turns the glycogen into glucose again and sends it to your tissues through the blood stream. The liver makes bile, which helps to digest fats and which is stored in the gall bladder. It manufactures many special enzymes. It destroys worn-out red blood cells. It produces the substances which cause the blood to clot. It is really a very busy factory.

But too much fat can interfere with the work of the liver and the red blood cells. So, most of the fat you digest is picked up in the small intestine by special ducts; it is then carried through a system of narrow tubes, called lymph vessels, until it reaches a large vein which lies under the left collar bone. There it enters the blood stream.

Lymph is a colorless liquid, similar to plasma. It is found all over the body. Apart from carrying fat, it helps to supply the cells and tissues with fluid, and it is another line of defense against infection. Throughout the lymph stream there are special filters called lymph nodes, in which bacteria are trapped and destroyed.

How Your Heart Works for You 6

Until about three centuries ago, physicians had many strange theories to explain what the heart does. The blood, they thought, carried noble spirits or sooty fumes, although nobody could quite explain what these were; and the heart was believed to cool the blood. Some physicians even thought that certain vessels in the body carried air, not blood, and they called these vessels *arteries*, which means air pipes.

Then in 1628 an English doctor named William Harvey published a book in which he described how the blood is driven around the body by the heart AS IT WERE, IN A CIRCLE. These are Harvey's own words. He had them printed in capital letters just as they are printed here, because the idea was so new and so different from the old ideas which were being taught.

He attacked the doctors who believed the arteries were filled with air; and he showed beyond any doubt that the arteries carried blood all over the body *away from* the heart, and that other vessels called veins carried the blood *back to* the heart.

William Harvey was a great scientist. But his book was only the beginning of our knowledge of the blood and the heart. Microscopes were not available in those days. So he used a magnifying glass to examine the bodies of animals and insects. This was not powerful enough to let him see how the blood, in its circle around the body, passed from the arteries to the veins. He could only guess, and his guess was proved right a few years after he died.

He did not know that the blood carried oxygen through the arteries, for oxygen was not discovered until 150 years later. And he could not know that the real work of the blood is to nourish all the living cells of the body, for cells were only discovered more than 200 years later.

In the first chapter of his book, William Harvey tells how he felt when he first began to study the heart. Everything happened so rapidly, he wrote, "that I was almost tempted to think that the motion of the heart was

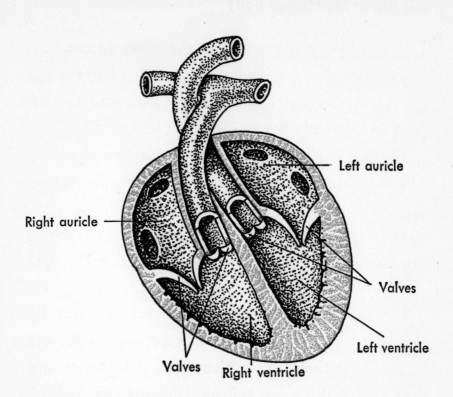

Right auricle

Left auricle

Valves

Left ventricle

Valves   Right ventricle

The heart, shown above, is a hollow muscle with four chambers and four sets of valves.

only to be comprehended by God." But, in time, he learned how the heart works. Today we can explain it quite simply, although we still do not know what causes it to work as it does.

The heart is shaped somewhat like a cone, tilted to one side with the point downward. It lies above the diaphragm between the two lungs, almost in the middle of the chest.

All About the Human Body

If you look at a drawing of the inside of the heart you will see that it is divided, from top to bottom, into two parts. For convenience, these are called the left heart and the right heart.

The left heart is divided across into two chambers. The top chamber is called the left auricle; the bottom chamber is called the left ventricle.

The right heart is divided in the same way, and its two chambers have similar names: the top is the right auricle, the bottom is the right ventricle.

The heart is built of muscle. All muscles work by contracting, which means that they become smaller and tighter. Then they relax, which means that they resume their normal shape and become long and not so hard. You can see how this happens if you tighten the muscle in the upper part of your arm, the biceps, and then let it relax.

Not all the muscle tissue of the heart tightens at the same time. First one part tightens, then another. This tightening, of course, makes the chambers inside the heart smaller, and anything inside the chambers is given a powerful squeeze.

But the chambers are filled with blood. To understand

what happens to this blood we need to watch the heart at work.

The vessels which carry blood to the heart are called veins. All the blood from your head, your arms, your legs and your intestines is collected in two large veins which go to the top chamber on the right side of your heart——the right auricle.

This blood has completed its task of providing the cells with nourishment and oxygen. Now, on its way back to the heart, it has collected the waste carbon dioxide which your cells do not need.

But you must not think of the venous blood (as the blood in the veins is called) as "bad" blood because it carries waste. Some of it, which came from the intestines and passed through the liver, has collected a supply of fresh nourishment. It also carries several special chemicals without which your heart could not work.

Even the waste carbon dioxide is put to use before we breathe it out. It helps to control the action of the heart and the lungs.

The venous blood enters the top chamber on the right side of the heart, the right auricle. As soon as the auricle is filled, it contracts, squeezing the blood into the lower chamber or the right ventricle. Between these two chambers there is a sort of trap door called a valve, which allows the blood to flow only in one direction. This valve stays open until the ventricle is filled. Then it closes tightly, so that the blood cannot return to the top chamber.

As soon as the ventricle is filled, it contracts, and the blood is squeezed into a large blood vessel leading from the heart to the lungs. Blood vessels carrying blood away from the heart are called arteries, and this one is called the pulmonary or lung artery. It has two branches, one going to each lung.

In the lungs the venous blood exchanges its carbon dioxide for oxygen. Now it is called oxygenated blood. And it is bright red. Venous blood is much darker red.

Now two veins from each lung carry the oxygenated blood back to the heart. This time the blood flows into the top chamber on the left side of the heart—the left auricle.

As soon as this fills, it contracts, and the blood is squeezed into the lower chamber, the left ventricle. Between these two chambers there is a valve, just as there is between the chambers of the right heart. It looks like

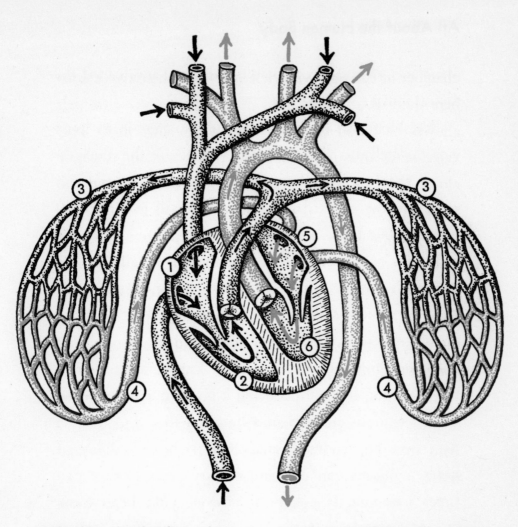

1. Blood from head and arms, legs and intestines enters right auricle and is squeezed into right ventricle.

2. Right ventricle squeezes blood through pulmonary artery to the lungs.

3. Venous blood enters lungs.

4. Oxygenated blood leaves lungs and flows back through pulmonary vein to the heart.

5. The blood enters the left auricle and is squeezed into the left ventricle.

6. Left ventricle forces the blood into the aorta from which it flows to all parts of the body.

the mitre, or headdress, of a bishop, and it is called the mitral valve.

The blood has now reached the last stage in its journey through the heart. The left ventricle is the strongest of all the four chambers because when it contracts it must squeeze so hard that the blood will be driven all around your body in about sixty seconds.

If you could see a slow motion film of all that has happened to the heart so far, you would notice that the two sides of the heart work together. The two top chambers contract; then they relax, and the two bottom chambers contract and then relax. This action produces the heartbeat. In a human being it happens about seventy times a minute, more than a hundred thousand times a day. By comparison, a canary's heart beats a thousand times a minute; an elephant's heart beats twenty-five times a minute. If you have a fever, your heart beats faster. It also beats faster when you are excited; but it usually beats more slowly when you sleep.

When the blood leaves the left ventricle it must travel to every living cell in your body. For this reason, the blood vessel which carries it away from your heart is very strong and thick——about an inch in diameter.

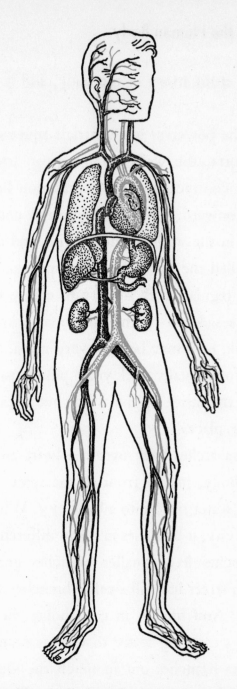

Arteries carry blood all over the body away from the heart.
The main artery, called the aorta, arches back over the heart.

This is the main artery of the body, and it is called the aorta.

When the powerful left ventricle squeezes the blood into the aorta, the walls of this great artery expand. Then they contract, and the contraction helps to push the blood onward. The expansion and contraction set up a wave in the walls of the arteries, and this wave or throb is called the pulse. In a well person, the pulse is strong and regular, with seventy to eighty beats a minute. With a sick person the pulse may slow down and appear weak, or it may become very rapid. For convenience, doctors usually feel your pulse just below the thumb, on the inside of the wrist, but it can be felt in many other places.

The aorta arches back over the heart and then goes down the body, just in front of the spine. It is almost like a great water main into a busy city. When the main reaches the city, it branches in many different directions. These branches have smaller branches going to each street. Each street has still smaller branches which go to each house. And finally, in each house there are even smaller pipes carrying water to various rooms.

The aorta branches out in much the same way. Its first branches are quite small though. They are called

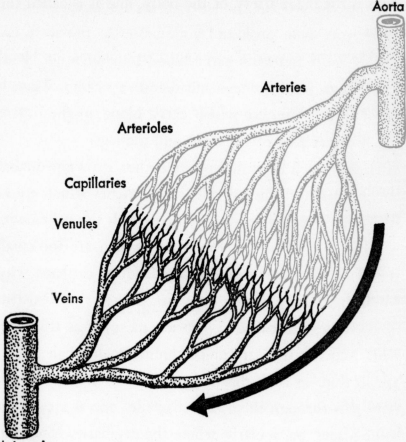

Blood always flows in one direction from the aorta.

the coronary arteries, and they go right back to the heart. Without food and oxygen to provide energy, the hard-working heart muscle could not perform its task of driving blood around your body.

All About the Human Body

From the arch of the aorta, branches carry blood to your arms, your neck and your head. As the aorta descends, more branches carry blood to your lungs, your diaphragm, your kidneys and digestive system. Then it divides into branches which carry blood to the organs in the lower part of the body and the legs.

Each branch has still more branches, growing smaller and smaller until they divide into branches which are so small that you can hardly see them with the naked eye.

These break up into tiny tubes which are too small to be seen without a microscope, which explains why William Harvey could only guess that they existed. These tubes are called capillaries, meaning as thin as a hair. Actually they are much thinner than a hair. They are so thin, in fact, that the red cells of the blood can only pass through them in Indian file, one at a time. In some places, particularly where the capillaries bend, the red cells have to bend almost double to pass through.

It is only from the capillaries that food and oxygen can reach the tissues and the cells of the body. The walls of the arteries, and even of the arterioles, are too thick to allow anything to escape through them. But the walls of the capillaries are only one cell in thickness, so that tiny particles of food and molecules of oxygen can slip through and reach the cells near by. It is the network of capillaries, covering your entire body, that keeps you alive and healthy. All the nourishment you need to provide energy and to enable you to grow, seeps out to your cells through millions of these tiny tubes.

As the blood gives up its food and oxygen, it collects carbon dioxide and other waste products of the cells. In a marvelous way, these substances seep into the capillaries.

Now the blood is ready to pass into the veins, to be carried back to the heart.

The capillaries join to form tiny veins, called venules. These join, forming larger and larger veins. Finally all the venous blood is carried into the two great veins which enter the top chamber on the right side of the heart——the right auricle. And there, with scarcely any rest, the circle of the blood starts again.

How You Breathe 7

When you breathe in, it is to supply your blood with fresh oxygen, which enables the cells to produce energy. When you breathe out, you get rid of the waste carbon dioxide which your blood has carried away from the cells.

Also, when you breathe out, you are helping your body to keep cool by expelling a little water vapor. But this can be done in other ways——by sweating, for example. So the really important work you do when you breathe is exchanging carbon dioxide for oxygen.

There are two ways in which you can breathe. As you sit reading this book, you are hardly aware that you are breathing at all. But you are breathing very lightly through your nose about sixteen times a minute.

If you were to drop this book, though, and run

around the block at top speed, you might soon find yourself puffing and panting. By this rapid breathing through the mouth you provide your blood with the extra oxygen you need when you use up a lot of energy in a short time.

However, your mouth is not really designed for breathing, as you have probably discovered for yourself on very cold days. Then you find yourself keeping your mouth tightly closed because you can feel the coldness of the air. Even your teeth feel the cold. On extremely cold days you often lower your chin so that your mouth is protected by your coat collar or scarf. The reason is that the cold air passing through your mouth does not have a chance to become warmed, and it actually causes a shock to your lungs.

But you can breathe quite comfortably through your nose, even though your nose may feel cold on the outside. This is because inside your nose there are a great many small blood vessels which swell with blood when the air is cold. As the air passes them on its way to the lungs, it is warmed to body temperature.

There is one slight disadvantage to this. When the small blood vessels swell, they cause more of a sticky liquid called mucus to be produced in your nose. That is why on a cold morning you have to blow your nose so often. The same effect is caused by a cold in the head.

Mucus moistens and protects the delicate tissue which lines all the air passages. Along with the hairs in the nostrils, it traps particles of dust, preventing them from reaching the lungs.

Your nostrils are separated by a partition called the septum. In the lower part of the nose this is made of cartilage, a flexible kind of bone. The upper part is real bone. So you can pull the bottom part of your nose from side to side, but you cannot move the top part at all.

High up, at the back of the nose, is a small recess or pocket, which is the center of your sense of smell. When you smell anything special, like food or perfume, you give a little sniff; and this sniffing carries the odor up into the pocket. The nerves of your sense of smell are very close to the brain, and go directly up into it.

The two air passages from your nose lead to the back of the mouth. Here are the adenoids, which are simply a mass of soft tissue filled with lymph nodes. Their purpose is to trap any infection which enters through your nose when you breathe.

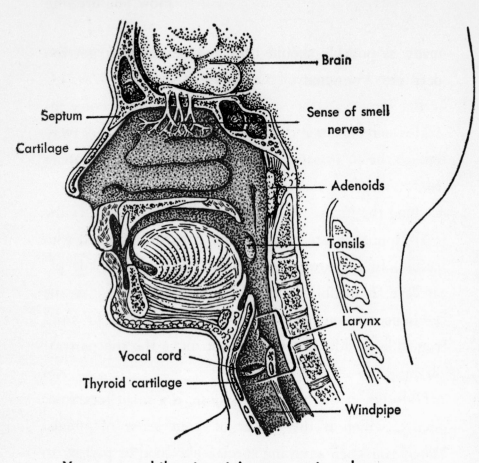

Your nose and throat contain many parts and serve many purposes.

The tonsils, at the back of the mouth, consist of the same kind of tissue and have the same purpose.

Thus, the hairs and mucus of your nose, your adenoids and tonsils, make up a kind of filter system. The air is full of harmful bacteria, and it is important that as many as possible should be killed before they get too deep into your body.

But sometimes the adenoids or the tonsils become infected and inflamed. Then parts must be snipped away because they interfere with your breathing. Snipping away the tissue is a very simple operation.

Leading from the back of the mouth, in front of the esophagus which carries your food, is the air passage to your lungs.

The first section, near the top of the throat, is the larynx, or voice box. Within the larynx are the vocal cords. These are two thin membranes arranged in a V shape. When you are not speaking or singing the two sides of the V are wide apart. But when you speak or sing the two sides are brought together and tightened by muscles. Air passing between them causes them to vibrate and create different sounds. Women and children have rather short vocal cords, so the sounds they make are high in pitch. Men have longer vocal cords, and as a result their voices are deeper.

Below the larynx is the windpipe. It is about four or five inches long, and the air passage inside it is about the same diameter as your forefinger. The wall of the windpipe is very strong. It is made even stronger by sixteen—sometimes as many as twenty—rings of cartilage. These make it look like the armored pipes in a jet plane. Yet, despite its great strength, the windpipe is quite elastic, so that you can turn your head from side to side and look up or down with ease.

For further safety, the larynx and the windpipe are guarded by several groups of strong cartilage. You can feel one cartilage in particular near the top of your neck, under your chin. It is formed of two large plates, rather like wings, which join in front and make a pointed ridge. It acts as a shield for the larynx, and it also looks like a shield; and this is the meaning of its name, the thyroid cartilage. The pointed ridge in the front, though, has its own name, the Adam's apple.

Near the thyroid cartilage is one of the most important glands in your body, the thyroid gland. It consists of two large lobes, about two inches long, lying on either side of the windpipe. It helps to control your growth and your energy. But, although it is so close to the windpipe, it does not directly affect your breathing.

At the back of each lobe there are two very much smaller glands—making four in all—called the parathyroid glands. These control the amount of calcium in

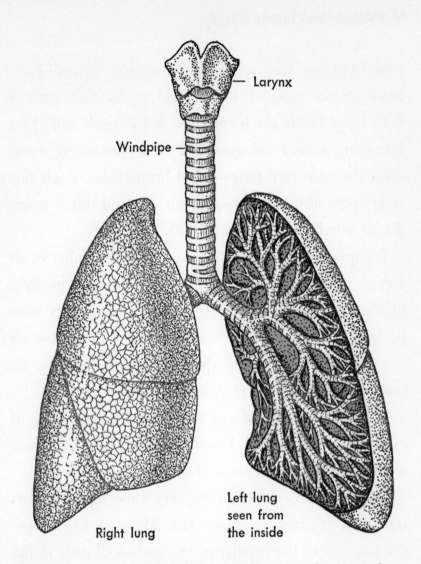

Larynx

Windpipe

Right lung

Left lung
seen from
the inside

The lungs bring blood and air together to exchange carbon dioxide for oxygen.

your blood, or (as scientists prefer to say) the calcium balance.

When the windpipe enters your chest, it divides into

two branches like a Y turned upside down. These branches are called the bronchial tubes. One goes to each lung. Inside the lungs they divide again and again, becoming smaller and smaller like the branches of a tree, until they are tiny twigs called bronchioles. Each tiny twig opens into a little bag, or air sac; and this is where the air you breathe in finally ends its journey.

It is practically impossible to count the number of air sacs in the lungs. Some scientists say there are nearly a billion. You can see, therefore, that the air sacs must be very, very small, and that the walls around the air sacs must be exceedingly thin. The walls, in fact, are built of a single layer of cells.

Surrounding the walls of the air sacs is a network of capillaries, the smallest blood vessels. These also have walls that are the thickness of a single layer of cells.

So, at last, blood and air are very close together, separated by just two layers of cells. Although blood cannot pass out of the capillaries, the carbon dioxide in the blood can pass easily. It just seeps through to the air sacs. At the same time, oxygen seeps out of the air sacs, into the capillaries. And so the exchange takes place.

But, you are probably asking, why does the exchange take place?

It is made possible by a substance called hemoglobin. This is a chemical compound containing iron, which gives the red blood cells their red color. Hemoglobin is a remarkable substance. It seems to like both carbon dioxide and oxygen; or, a scientist would say, it has an affinity for each of these two gases. As the red cells travel through the tissues of your body, the hemoglobin collects the waste carbon dioxide. Then, when the red blood cells reach your lungs, the hemoglobin gives away the carbon dioxide in exchange for oxygen, which it likes just as much.

Now the blood is oxygenated, and it flows from the capillaries in the lungs to larger and larger blood vessels, returning to the heart, where it can be pumped around your body. The air in your lungs is now loaded with carbon dioxide, and you are ready to breathe it out and breathe in a fresh supply of oxygen.

This is how the exchange takes place inside your lungs. But it is important to see how your lungs work— that is, how they enable you to breathe in and out.

Your two lungs are much larger than most people think they are. They reach all the way from the root of your neck to your diaphragm, which is the fence of muscular tissue that divides your body in two parts.

They are shaped roughly like cones, pointed at the top and broad at the bottom.

Each lung is quite separate. If for some reason you could not breathe with one you could still breathe with the other. They are also slightly different in shape and appearance. Running across the outside are grooves, or fissures, which divide them into sections called lobes. The left lung has two lobes, the right lung three. The left lung is also a little smaller than the right. The reason for this is that the heart lies between the two lungs, but since it lies rather more on the left side the left lung is smaller to make room for it.

The inside of a lung is like a sponge, very light in weight because it has so many millions of air sacs. It is also very elastic. This means that your lungs can be stretched easily, but as soon as they are released they go back at once to their original shape.

Surrounding and guarding your lungs are twelve pairs of ribs. All are joined to your spine at the back and curve around your chest to form a strong cage. In front, the top seven pairs are connected to your breastbone by cartilage. The next three pairs are connected to the rib above. Because the last two pairs are left unconnected in front, they are often called the

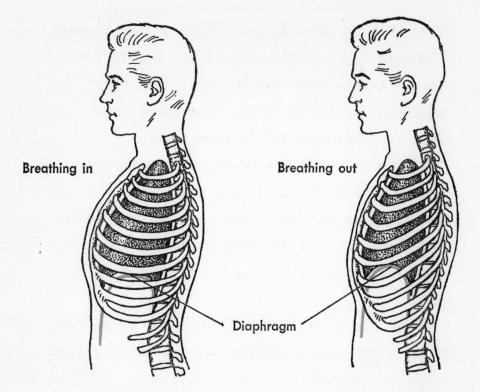

Breathing in

Breathing out

Diaphragm

As you breathe in, your diaphragm is pulled downward.

floating ribs. Your entire rib cage is flexible: special muscles can cause it to expand without any difficulty.

Your lungs do not suck in air by themselves. All the work is done for them by your strong diaphragm and the muscles of your rib cage.

When you breathe in, the muscles of your diaphragm contract, and the diaphragm is pulled downward. At the same time, the rib muscles pull the ribs upward and outward. Your chest becomes bigger; it has expanded. This causes your lungs to expand too; and the tiny air sacs inside your lungs also become a little bigger. Because there is now so much more space inside your lungs, air flows in to fill the extra space.

When you breathe out, exactly the opposite happens. The muscles of the diaphragm relax, and so do the muscles of the rib cage. Your chest becomes smaller. The elastic tissue of the lungs returns to its original shape, making the air sacs smaller, and the air is driven out.

Meanwhile, your blood has had time to do its work, giving away carbon dioxide and collecting a fresh supply of oxygen.

You can see from this how wonderfully well all the different parts of your body work together. Your heart, your lungs, your digestive system, your bones and your muscles——all help each other.

Even the air which is driven out of your lungs is put to use. As it passes your vocal chords you use it to talk and sing.

Kidneys, Hormones and Your Bad-tempered Spleen

Suppose you stand up straight, with your arms hanging down at your sides. Now imagine a line across your back from elbow to elbow. Your two kidneys are just about on this line, one on either side of your backbone. They are quite high in your back, just below the diaphragm, and they are protected by your last two ribs——the floating ribs. They are also protected by being enclosed in a mass of fat, which helps to support them in your body.

Your kidneys look like large beans. Perhaps it would be more accurate to put this the other way and say that some beans look like small kidneys and are therefore called kidney beans. In an adult the kidneys are

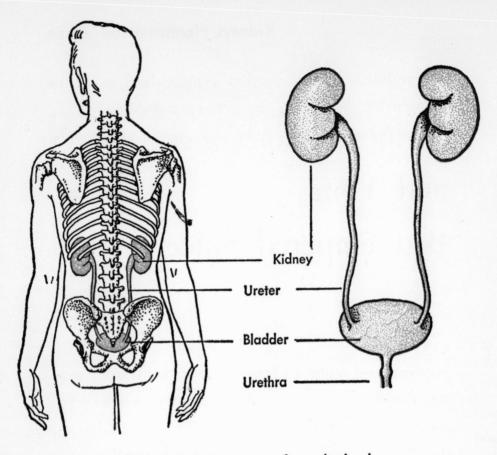

The urinary system seen from the back

about 4½ inches long, about 2½ inches wide and about 1½ inches thick.

Their work is very important. Yet, strangely enough, people can live perfectly normal lives with only one kidney and—stranger still—scientists have discovered that we can stay alive with only half a kidney, as long as this portion is healthy.

In a way, the kidneys are a part of your blood

system; but it is more usual to explain them as part of a system of their own, the urinary system.

You have seen that you must have oxygen, food and water in order to live. These substances are used by your body to produce energy and to build new cells. At the same time certain kinds of waste are produced which your body does not need. There is the waste of your food, which you pass out from your digestive system every day. There is the carbon dioxide which you breathe out.

There are also other waste products which are carried in your blood stream. Some of these would be dangerous if they stayed in your body too long. For example, a substance called urea is produced when the proteins of your food are broken down. This is a waste which must be eliminated.

Another waste which must be eliminated from the blood stream is called uric acid.

Another is water. You may wonder why this is so since your body needs water constantly.

First, some of the water you drink is used to dissolve wastes like urea and uric acid so that they can be carried out of your body easily.

Second, you can have more water in your body

than you need. You must get rid of this excess so that there is not too much liquid in your blood stream.

The task of the kidneys, then, is to take out of the blood stream waste substances like urea and uric acid, which are dissolved in water. In addition, your kidneys extract any water you do not need. They also keep guard over the balance of chemicals in your blood stream.

This work is so important that all your blood flows through your kidneys every few minutes. Yet, for safety, your kidneys have a large reserve. Only a small part—about one-sixth—is working at any time.

There are three tubes in the side of each kidney. One is a large artery, carrying the blood which is to be purified. The second is a large vein, carrying away the purified blood. The third tube, called a ureter, carries urine down to the bladder.

Inside the kidney, the artery divides into branches, and these branches spread and divide into still smaller branches, until eventually they become the smallest of all blood vessels: capillaries.

If you look at these capillaries under a microscope you will notice that they are not spread out in a net-

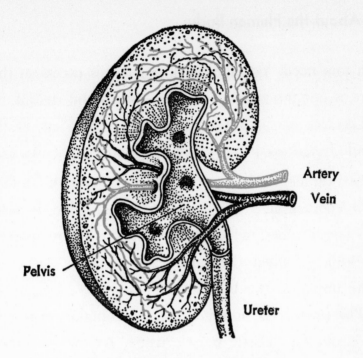

The right kidney seen from inside

work. Instead, about fifty of them have bunched together to form a compact little ball. Around the ball is a sort of cup, or capsule. Hanging down from the capsule is a tiny tube which forms a long loop, or tubule.

The whole of this structure is called a nephron. Each of your kidneys is composed of more than a million nephrons.

What happens in the nephron is that as the blood

travels through the ball of capillaries, water containing the waste substances is extracted from the blood and passes into the capsule.

Next, the water passes from the capsule into the long looped tubule. As it goes through the tubule, it becomes more concentrated, and it is now called urine. It passes into larger tubes, which empty into a hollow part of the kidney. Then the tubes called ureters carry the urine down to the bladder.

The bladder is simply a sac, or container, made of thick layers of elastic muscle tissue. At the bottom of the bladder there is an opening which, normally, is kept tightly closed by a ring of muscle called the bladder sphincter. When this muscle relaxes and opens, the urine passes through into a tube called the urethra, and leaves your body.

Learning to control the ring of muscle guarding the bladder is sometimes very difficult for young children. A baby cannot control the bladder sphincter at all, and therefore as soon as excess urine collects in the bladder it flows out, and the baby wets its diaper.

Sitting on top of each of the kidneys is a curious little structure which looks like a little pixie hat, about an inch and a half high. These are the adrenal glands, which means the glands over the kidneys. Occasionally you may see them called suprarenal glands, which has the same meaning.

Each adrenal gland consists of two parts: the cortex, which means a covering like the bark of a tree, and the medulla, which means the marrow, or center. (Other parts of the body are called cortex, or medulla, and this may lead to some confusion unless we say precisely which part of the body we mean.)

The medulla, or inside, of the adrenal glands produces a hormone called adrenalin, which affects the nervous system and the blood. The cortex of the adrenal glands produces a hormone called cortin, which controls the amount of salt in the blood. One of our most important modern drugs, cortisone, was first made from the cortex of the adrenal glands of certain animals. Now chemists can make it in their laboratories.

Hormones and How They Work

The hormones stimulate cells, tissues and organs in different parts of your body. In this way, they have a controlling effect on your growth and your energy. The hormone substances travel through your blood

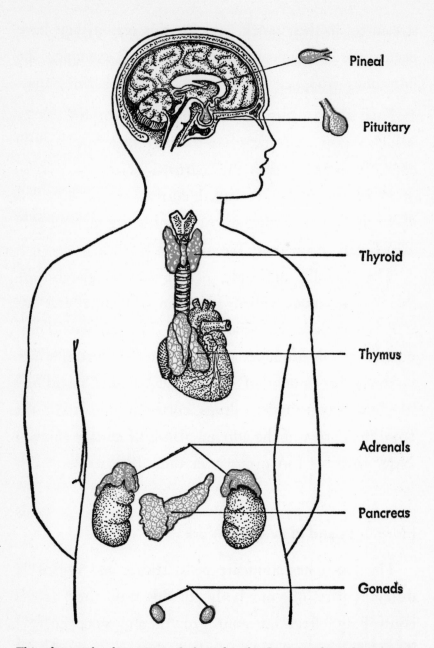

Pineal

Pituitary

Thyroid

Thymus

Adrenals

Pancreas

Gonads

This shows the location of the glands that produce hormones.

stream to do their work, and for this reason they have been called chemical messengers. For example, the hormones produced by your adrenal glands carry messages to your heart and to other parts of your body, although they are actually produced in the two little glands just over your kidneys.

There are several glands beside the adrenals which produce hormones. They are called the endocrine glands. Here is a list of them:

The *pituitary gland* is suspended from the base of the brain, like a cherry on a rather thick stalk. It is guarded by a strange formation of bone which looks like the kind of saddle used by Turkish horsemen. It is often called the master gland, because it appears to control the activity of all the glands in the endocrine system.

The *pineal body*, also, is in the skull, near the brain, and is usually considered to be part of the endocrine system. We know very little about it, though. It seems to work with the adrenal glands.

The *thyroid*, and the *parathyroids*, are endocrine glands. The *thymus*, in the upper part of the chest, helps to control the growth of children and later ceases to be active. The pancreas is dotted with groups of cells called the *Islets of Langerhans*, which produce a substance called insulin. This controls the use of sugar by the cells and regulates the amount of sugar in the blood. In addition, there are the special glands called the *gonads*, which are concerned with sex: the male *testes* and the female *ovaries*. Other hormones are produced by the body, but we still have to learn a great deal more about them.

The Spleen and How It Works

For many centuries the spleen was considered to be the organ of bad temper. We still use the word to mean ill humor, peevish temper, or spite.

Even today we know very little about the spleen. We can live without it quite comfortably. As far as I know, people who have had their spleens taken out are just as bad-tempered as they were before.

The spleen is fairly large; in a grown person it is about the size of the fist. It lies below the diaphragm, behind the stomach, and a little above the left kidney; and it is purplish-red in color. It holds a lot of blood, and it acts as a blood reservoir, releasing blood when you need it—for example, when you cut yourself badly.

Its most important work will probably surprise you: it destroys red blood cells. This work is done by both the spleen and the liver.

But red blood cells are so valuable. Why must they be destroyed?

The reason is that they wear out in about thirty days. When they are worn out, your body destroys them and uses the materials from which they are made to help make new red cells. Some of the materials are used for other purposes too.

This process goes on constantly.

Every second, your spleen and your liver destroy about ten million worn-out red blood cells.

These must be replaced, of course. Every second, therefore, about ten million new red blood cells come into existence. They are made, not in any one special organ, but throughout your body, inside your bones.

Your Amazing Bones 9

Your bones are the framework of your body. They give your body strength and rigidity, and they enable you to move from place to place without flopping over like a jellyfish.

They also protect your internal organs. The bones of your skull protect your brain. The ribs protect your lungs and heart, and to some extent your stomach, liver and kidneys. The pelvic bones protect organs in the lower part of the body.

Bones come in all shapes and sizes. There are long bones, like those in your arms and legs; short bones, like those in your fingers; flat bones, like the "wings" of your shoulders. Each one is designed for the work it has to do. Every bump or hollow on a bone has some purpose. Engineers who have studied bones are astounded by the marvelous way in which they are constructed.

Your bones started as cartilage long before you were born. Cartilage is tough but fairly soft. As the unborn baby develops, the cartilage ossifies. This means that calcium salts are deposited in it, turning it to hard bony substance.

The first to ossify are the clavicles, or collar bones, which you can feel above your chest, stretching on either side of your neck to your arms. The process of growing and hardening goes on until you are about twenty-five years old. By that time your bones are stronger, weight for weight, than iron.

It is easy to remember the number of bones in your body. Not counting the three tiny bones in each ear, there are exactly two hundred. Here, for reference, is a table of them.

	Number of bones
Skull	22
Hyoid bone	1
(in front of neck)	
Spinal column	26
Ribs	24
Breastbone	1
Arms and hands	64
Legs and feet	62

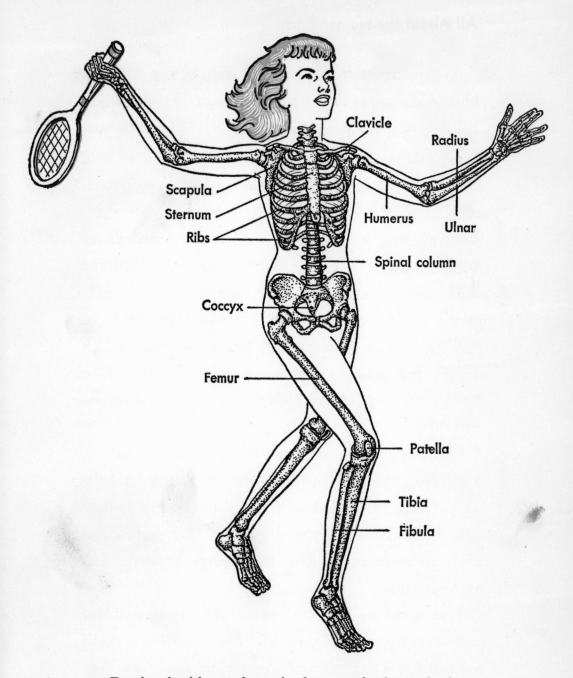

Clavicle

Radius

Scapula

Sternum

Ribs

Humerus

Ulnar

Spinal column

Coccyx

Femur

Patella

Tibia

Fibula

Two hundred bones form the framework of your body.

In addition, you have about twenty bones which are not considered true bones. They are called sesamoid bones, which means shaped like a flat seed. The best example is your kneecap, or patella. This slides over the front of your knee and protects it in certain positions, as when you kneel down.

If you look at one of the long bones, you will see that it consists of a long narrow portion, called the shaft, with a rounded head at each end. The outside of the shaft is covered with a strong skin called the periosteum. This contains many fine blood vessels which nourish the bone and give it its pinkish color. Like every other part of the body, bones must be supplied with blood.

Under the skin around the bone, there is a shell of hard bone, like ivory, which grows thicker around the middle of the shaft. Below this shell the bone is spongy in appearance. The little sponge-like holes are filled with red marrow. Most of this spongy bone tissue is near the ends.

This is where the millions of red blood cells are made every second of your life. Inside the bones, each red cell has a nucleus and can divide. Each one goes through several stages as it develops. Then, just as it is ready to join the other red cells in the blood stream, the nucleus disappears. Therefore, a red cell in the blood stream has no nucleus, cannot divide and cannot reproduce itself. Red cells multiply only inside the spongy marrow of your bones.

The very center of the bone is hollow and contains a different kind of marrow which is yellow and fatty. Here your bones store fat.

Bones are built so that they can grow as the body grows. At each end of the bone shaft, just below the head, there is a thin plate of cartilage. These are called the growth plates. This construction permits the shaft of the bone to grow in length without interfering with the heads. At the same time, the heads can grow without interfering with the shaft. When the growth plates ossify, the bones stop growing.

The bones of the top of your head—the cranium, which covers and protects the brain—are constructed in another way. They are flat and curved, and consist of a sandwich of hard bone with spongy bone in between. In grown people, the eight bones which form the cranium are very tightly locked together; but a baby has softer bones which are not yet ready to be locked into place. The spaces between the bones of

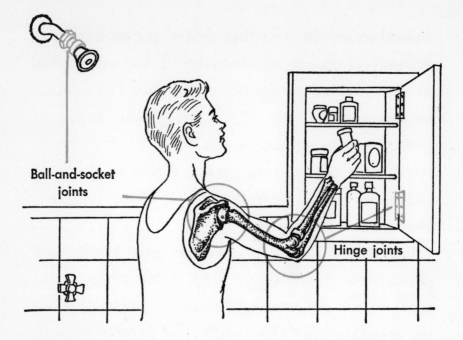

Ball-and-socket joints

Hinge joints

To allow free movement, bones are joined in different ways.

a baby's cranium are called fontanelles. There are six altogether, and you can often see two of them as slight hollows—one just above the forehead and one at the back of the head, near the top.

To make the strong framework of your body and to allow you to move freely, your bones are joined in several different ways. Some, like your elbows and knees, are joined by hinges. And some, like your hip joints and your shoulder joints, use a ball-and-socket arrangement. Hinge and ball-and-socket joints, and others which are rather similar, possess a layer of delicate membrane which makes a lubricating fluid so that the bones can move smoothly and without friction.

There are several joints—like those of the cranium—which cannot move at all when they are formed. In fact, your face and head are built up from twenty-two bones, but only the lower jaw, or mandible, can be moved. The mandible has two joints, one on either side

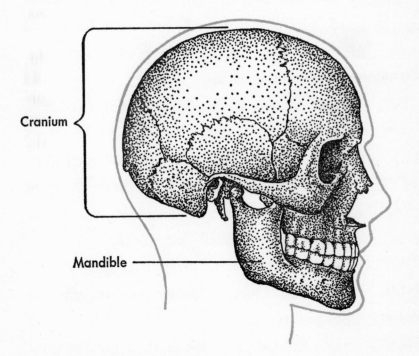

In the skull only the mandible, or lower jaw, can be moved.

of your face near your ears. These joints enable you to open your mouth to eat or talk or yawn. They also allow your lower jaw to move from side to side so that you can grind your food between your teeth.

One of the most remarkable mechanisms in your body is your spinal column or backbone. It is really a series of bones working together. Because of the shape and position of these bones, called vertebrae, you can turn your head without moving your body, and turn your body without moving your feet. They enable you to bend sideways, forward, and even backward to some degree. If your backbone were one solid bone, you could hardly move at all.

When a baby is born, its backbone is almost straight, except for a sort of hook at the bottom. As he grows older, several curves develop, which are perfectly normal. The backbone curves inward at the neck, outward below the shoulders, in again at the waist, out at the pelvis, and then sharply inward once more.

As you grow older, too, your backbone curves slightly to one side. Doctors believe this depends on whether you are right-handed or left-handed. Most people are right-handed. As a result they use the muscles on this side more, causing the spine to have a slight

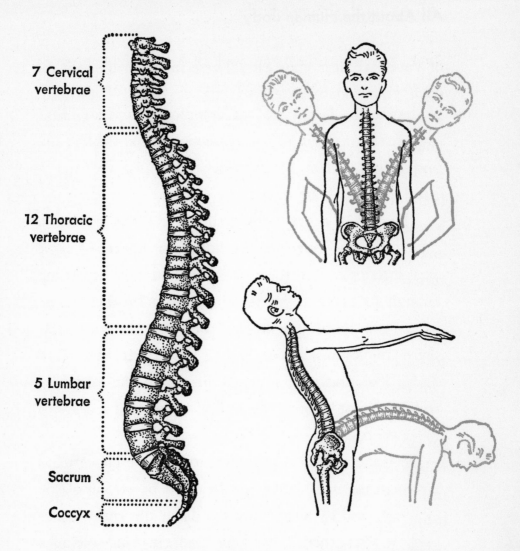

7 Cervical vertebrae

12 Thoracic vertebrae

5 Lumbar vertebrae

Sacrum

Coccyx

The most remarkable mechanism in your body is the spinal column.

curvature to the right. The opposite happens with left-handed people: the spine is pulled over to the left.

The spine is built up of thirty-three bones, or vertebrae; but sometimes you will find the number given as twenty-six. The reason is that in the lower part of the spine the bones are not completely separate. Five are joined, or fused, to form a section called the sacrum, and below this are four which are fused to form a small pointed bone called the coccyx.

The sacrum is very strong since the bones are fused. Above this the vertebrae are linked by fingers of bone that interlock. But these alone would not be strong enough to prevent the vertebrae from breaking loose when you move quickly; so, between the vertebrae, there are cushions of very strong fibrous cartilage called discs. The discs are attached firmly to the vertebrae and have just enough flexibility to allow for various movements.

To make the backbone even stronger, each vertebra is tied to the ones above and below it by strong elastic ligaments and by small muscles. Then the entire backbone is strengthened by long ligaments and complex groups of muscles which guard it and control it. This arrangement permits you to move freely and without danger of any vertebra slipping out of place.

The very first vertebra, high up at the back of the neck, supports your head. It is very simple—just a ring

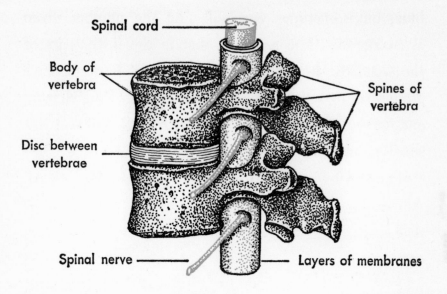

Spinal cord

Body of vertebra

Spines of vertebra

Disc between vertebrae

Spinal nerve

Layers of membranes

The spinal cord is protected by bone and layers of membranes.

of bone on which your head can rock up and down. It enables you to nod your head when you say "Yes!"

The second vertebra enables you to turn your head from side to side. And so you can shake your head when you say "No!"

Each vertebra has a large hole in the center. Lined up, one on the other, they form a continuous passage, or canal, for the spinal cord.

The spinal cord is the central pathway between your brain and practically every part of your body. If it is damaged, the results can be extremely serious. For this reason it is protected in several ways. It is sheathed in three separate membranes. It is surrounded by a special fluid, called the spinal fluid, which acts as a shock absorber. And, in addition, it is protected by the bony vertebrae with their armor of sharp strong spines. These are the spines you can feel down the middle of your back, which give the spinal column its name.

Your Muscles and   *10*
Your Skin

If you look closely at a skeleton in a museum, you will see that it is strung together by wires. To make it appear as if it is standing, it is supported by several rods. If the rods are taken away, it simply collapses.

You do not collapse because the bones of your skeleton are connected by joints and ligaments and supported by muscles. Sometimes a person will collapse, though, if he has been exerting himself too much, or when he has stayed awake too long. Then he has to sit down or lie down. His muscles have become tired of supporting him, and they need to rest.

There are more than 600 muscles in the human body. In an adult they weigh two and a half times as much as all of the bones together. The muscles are the flesh which gives your body its basic shape. Most important of all, they give you the power of movement.

Like any other part of the body, a muscle is built of cells. These cells are of a special kind, long and slender. Usually several cells fuse to form a unit called a muscle fiber. The remarkable thing about muscle fibers is that they can contract, or grow shorter.

A muscle consists of many bundles of long, slender muscle fibers. When the fibers are in their normal position, or relaxed, the muscle itself is relaxed. When the fibers contract, the muscle contracts. It grows shorter.

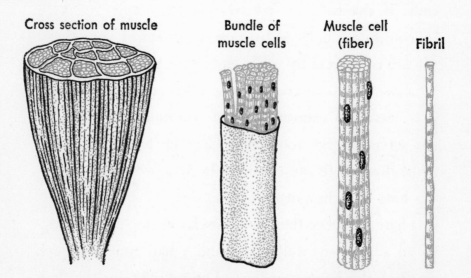

Cross section of muscle   Bundle of muscle cells   Muscle cell (fiber)   Fibril

A muscle consists of bundles of muscle cells called muscle fibers. Each cell or fiber is composed of delicate fibrils.

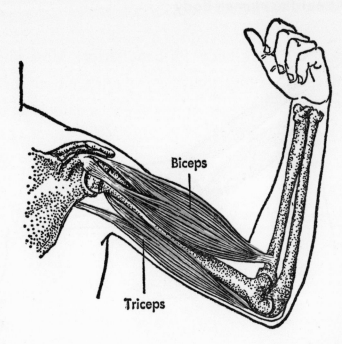

Biceps

Triceps

As you flex your arm, the biceps contracts and draws your forearm upward. At the same time the triceps relaxes.

Usually a muscle is attached between two bones. When the muscle is relaxed, nothing happens to the two bones. But as soon as the muscle contracts, the bones move.

Take a look at that muscle called the biceps which is in the front of your upper arm. Although you cannot see this, it is also attached to your forearm. When you flex your arm, this muscle bulges under your skin. It contracts, and as it does this, it draws your forearm upward.

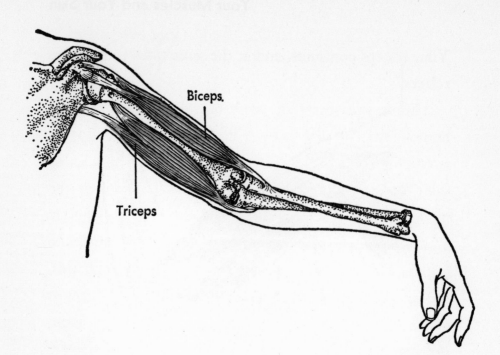

When the triceps contracts, the forearm is drawn downward.

But it is not enough to have a muscle which pulls your forearm up. You need a muscle which pulls the forearm down. So underneath the upper part of your arm, there is another powerful muscle called the triceps. This works in the opposite direction to the biceps. When the triceps contracts, the forearm is drawn downward.

Flexing your forearm, therefore, is a double action. Your biceps contracts; your triceps relaxes at the same time. Lowering your forearm is a double action too.

Your triceps contracts, and at the same time your biceps relaxes.

This is the secret of most of the muscles in your body. They work together, in pairs and in groups. It is true of the muscles of your legs and the muscles of your fingers, and the six muscles which control the movements of each of your eyes. No single muscle works alone. Whatever work it does, there must be a muscle to do the opposite. But even more than this, the simplest movement brings into action whole groups of muscles. Some of them may be far removed from the part of the body which seems to be doing all the work. For example, if you pull on a rope, your arm muscles are helped by the muscles of your back and your legs and even your toes.

When a muscle contracts, it becomes shorter in length but thicker in the middle. The same thing happens to the bundle of fibers. In turn, it happens to the entire muscle. That is why the biceps bulges when you flex your arm.

Normally when a muscle contracts, only some of the bundles of muscle fibers are called into action. This is because most of the work we do requires only a fairly small effort. But if we do particularly hard work,

As a man pulls himself up by rope, he uses the muscles of the
arms, the back and the legs.

more and more of the bundles of fibers are called into action. As a result the muscle becomes bigger and harder when it contracts. So, by work or by exercise, you can develop your muscles and make them strong.

We do not need very big, overdeveloped muscles. Indeed, they can become so big that they get in the way of other muscles and slow down our movements. A man who has developed enormous muscles for weight lifting is not likely to be a star tennis player. Athletes have strong muscles, but—even more important—their muscle reactions are quick, and all their muscles work in harmony.

In cold weather your skin muscles tighten a little. This causes little bumps or goose pimples to appear. All over your body you have very fine hairs, so fine that you are hardly aware of most of them. These hairs grow out of tiny bulbs under the skin. Attached to the side of each hair is a tiny muscle. When your skin is cold on a frosty day, these muscles contract and the fine hairs stand on end. This is part of your body's effort to keep you warm. At the same time, the hair bulbs are pushed up under the skin so that you can actually see them. They look like little bumps. You may have noticed that the hair on the fur of cats and dogs stands on end when they are cold. Birds try to keep themselves warm in a similar way, by fluffing out their feathers.

The fine hairs on your body are very useful. Close to each one there is a nerve ending called a touch spot. When an insect crawls over your skin, it disturbs the little hairs, alerting the touch spots; and you feel a

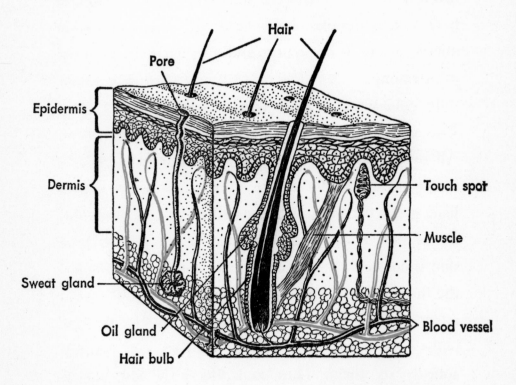

A cross section of the skin as seen through the microscope.

ticklish sensation which warns you to brush the insect off before it does you any harm.

Your hair also protects you in other ways. Your eyelashes keep dust out of your eyes; the hair inside your nose helps to filter the air you breathe; and the hair on your head protects your skull and brain.

There is no hair on your fingertips and they are sensitive for a different reason.

If you hold your palm up and examine the tips of your fingers, you can see that the skin consists of numerous little ridges which form a pattern of rings and curves. These little ridges are extremely sensitive, and you use them constantly to find out how things feel.

If you could look at a small piece of skin under a microscope, you would see that skin really consists of two skins. They are tightly joined but quite different. The outer one is called the epidermis. It is simply a protective covering for the true skin underneath, which is called the dermis.

The epidermis is not really sensitive. You may have noticed that sometimes when you scratch yourself only a white mark is left. It doesn't bleed, and it scarcely hurts. The reason is that you have only scraped the epidermis; and the white scratch itself is merely made up of dead cells. The nerves and blood vessels are in the true skin below, the dermis.

The epidermis, then, is the skin of your skin. It takes all the wear and tear of daily living. It keeps out moisture and bacteria.

Under a microscope you can see that the two skins are interlocked in a line that looks like an endless mountain range, with high peaks and deep valleys. This pattern of ridges causes what we call a fingerprint.

No two people have the same fingerprint. So a man's fingerprint is the best possible identification. If a criminal tried to change his fingerprints by rubbing them off with sandpaper, he would have to remove the pattern in both the epidermis and the dermis. This would be agonizing. Even if he had his fingerprints removed by surgery, it would only make the police very suspicious of him. They would guess at once that only a criminal would have reasons to hide his identity.

Your Nerves, Your Brain, Your Ears and Your Eyes

When you go for a walk, you don't have to worry about what your legs and feet are doing. Your brain takes care of all your movements, and you walk along the street without any difficulty.

But walking is really a marvelous achievement. When a baby begins to walk, in the first year of his life, it is hard for his brain to control his legs and balance his body. That is why he stumbles and falls so often.

Even an adult may have difficulty learning how to move in a new way. Some of the leg strokes in swimming require a great deal of practice before they are mastered. Many people have difficulty learning to dance. At first they have to think where to put each foot. Sometimes they feel as confused as the centipede which was confronted with the question:

> ... "Pray, which leg goes after which?"
> This worked her mind to such a pitch
> She lay distracted in a ditch
> Considering HOW to run.

The brain takes care of all our movements. But how does this happen? How can your brain, in the top of your head, tell your legs and arms what to do?

Nobody can answer these questions completely because no one understands how the human brain works. Hundreds of learned books have been written about it, but it is still a mystery. Even such an everyday act as reading is so complicated that no scientist can explain just what happens in the brain as you read the printed words.

In some ways the human brain is like an enormous telephone exchange, with millions and millions of telephone wires going out from its switchboards. In the human body the "switchboards" are built of special kinds of cells called nerve cells. The "telephone wires" are called nerve fibers. They reach to every part of your body. Where each nerve fiber ends, it spreads out into a number of very small branches called an end plate or, more simply, a nerve ending. The nerve fiber and the nerve ending are actually parts of the nerve cell.

Suppose you are about to pick up a small object—say, a pin. This is not a hard thing to do, yet you will have to move many parts of your body to do it. If you go through the motion of picking up a pin from the floor, you will see that you have to move your eyes, your head, your neck, your shoulders, your back, your hips, your legs, your feet, and—in particular—your arm, your hand and your fingers!

Your bones cannot move by themselves, of course. They are moved by muscles which are attached from one bone to another. The movement takes place only when the muscles contract, or become shorter.

In the same way, muscles cannot contract by themselves. They must be told to contract by your brain. A message must come to each muscle from your brain switchboard. This message travels along the telephone

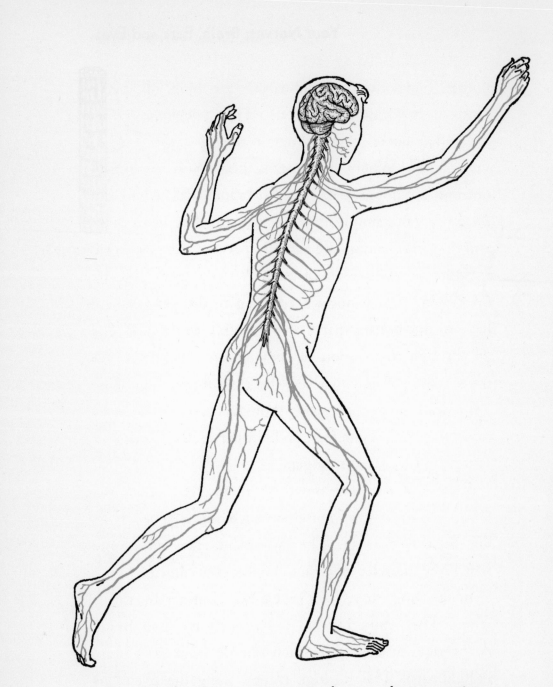

The central nervous system controls our voluntary actions.

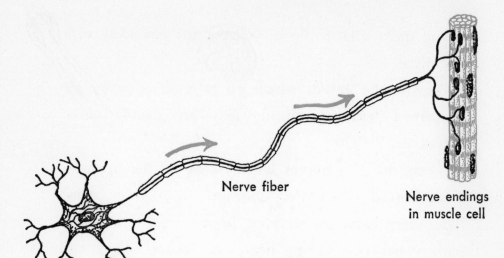

Nerve fiber

Nerve endings
in muscle cell

Nerve cell

A simplified diagram of the pathway from the brain to a muscle

wire, or nerve fiber, going to the muscle. When the message reaches the nerve ending in the muscle, the muscle obeys your brain and contracts.

Hundreds of thousands of nerve fibers go to the muscles in your arms and hands. As you reach down to pick up the pin, your brain sends messages to the muscles in perfect order, choosing exactly the right muscles to contract and also the right muscles to relax. Finally, your thumb and forefinger tighten around the pin and pick it up. Then, once again in perfect order, the messages come from your brain to your muscles telling them what to do as you put the pin away in a safe place.

Because the nerves which go to your muscles are concerned with movement, they are called motor nerves.

There are also nerves which work in the opposite way. Instead of carrying messages from your brain, they carry messages to your brain. They are called sensory nerves, meaning nerves of feeling. They tell

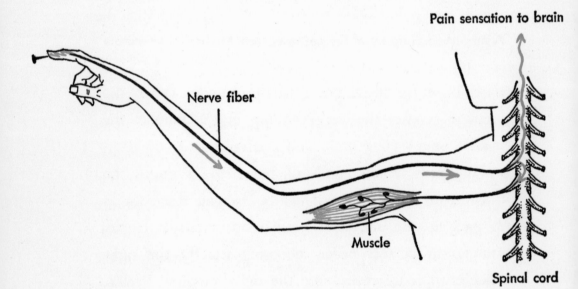

Pain sensation to brain

Nerve fiber

Muscle

Spinal cord

A nerve fiber carries the message to the arm muscle which pulls back even before the pain sensation reaches the brain.

you of heat and cold, for example, and wetness and dryness.

To understand how the sensory nerves work, imagine that before you pick up the pin, it scratches your hand slightly.

As the point of the pin scratches your hand, it disturbs the endings of pain nerves in your skin. At once messages are sent along the nerve fibers up to your brain, telling what is happening. Pain usually means that damage is being done to the cells and tissues of your body, and your brain must know about it so that the damage can be stopped if possible.

But on the way up to your brain the sensory nerve passes through a sort of miniature telephone exchange with its own switchboard. Here it passes the bad news about the pin to motor nerves which are near by. Immediately—even before you have had time to feel pain—these motor nerves leap into action. Messages are sent down the motor nerve fibers; muscles contract; bones move; and you snatch your hand away from the sharp point before the pin can do any more damage. This is called a reflex action. It happens before your brain knows what has hurt you.

A fraction of a second later, when the pain message reaches your brain, many things happen. You probably exclaim, "Ouch!" Then you look at the scratch to see how serious it is. Your eyes are sensory organs, and they send messages to your brain describing the scratch in detail. Then perhaps the pin drops, and you hear the faint tinkle as it falls on the floor. Your ears, also, are sensory organs, and they send a message to your brain telling it where the pin has fallen. Now you reach down to pick up the pin; and your motor nerves go to work, activating your muscles. But the sensory nerve endings in your fingers are still busy. They feel the coldness and the hardness of the pin, its shape and its size. These messages tell your brain that you are actually picking up a pin and not a coin or a piece of paper.

We are conscious of many of the things we do such as moving about, writing or reading. These activities are called voluntary, and they are controlled by the Voluntary, or Central Nervous System.

But there are many other activities of which we are not conscious, and these must go on whether we are awake or asleep. The heart, the lungs, the digestive system, for example, must work twenty-four hours a

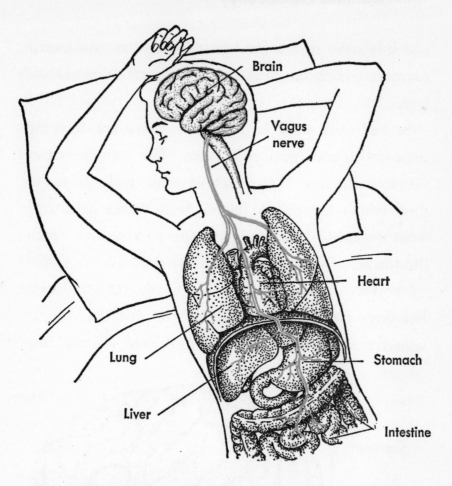

Even while you are asleep, the nerves direct such bodily
activities as breathing and digestion.

day; and their activities are controlled by the Involun-
tary, or Autonomic Nervous System.

One of its most important nerves is the Vagus nerve,
which originates at the base of the brain. Vagus comes
from a Latin root meaning a wanderer, or vagabond;

and this nerve travels through the chest and abdominal cavities, sending out branches to the vital organs of the body.

So, all over your body, nerve fibers are carrying messages to and from your brain. The activity is tremendous because every part of your body is under your brain's control. A famous writer once calculated what it would take to build a telephone exchange which did the same work as the brain. The equipment would fill six skyscrapers, each as big as the Empire State Building; the cables containing the telephone wires would weigh several hundred tons; and, to cool the

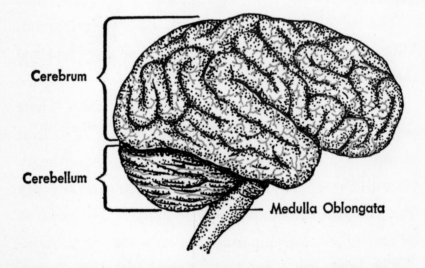

Cerebrum

Cerebellum

Medulla Oblongata

In the human brain the cerebrum is larger in proportion to body size than in any other animal.

equipment, we would need all the water in the Hudson River.

You can see from the drawing on page 112 what the human brain looks like. It grows quickly from the time you are born until you are about four or five. It continues to grow, not quite so quickly, until you are about twenty. When it has finished growing, it weighs a little less than three pounds. Only two animals have brains heavier than ours—elephants and some whales. The elephant's brain is about three times heavier, and the brains of certain very large whales are five times heavier. For their size, though, human beings have larger brains than any other creature.

The size of the brain, in fact, is not very important. What is important is the development of the brain and the ways it can be used. Scientists have discovered that the brains of almost all human beings look alike. There seems to be no difference between the brain of a great genius like Einstein and the brain of the most ordinary person. Perhaps, to be more accurate, I should say that scientists have been able to find no difference so far.

The brain has many parts, three of greatest importance: the cerebrum, which is the largest part; the cerebellum, which means the little brain; and the medulla oblongata, which is the part of the brain leading to the spinal cord.

In the human body, the cerebrum is much larger, in proportion to body size, than in any other animal. It is the center of sight, hearing, taste, smell, memory and intelligence. Because man's cerebrum is so highly developed, he can do a vast number of things which other animals cannot do. The cerebellum and the medulla oblongata are much alike in human beings and highly developed animals. They control movements and are responsible for keeping the body working.

Your Ears and How They Work

The sounds you hear must make an amazing journey through your ears. It is a journey of only about two inches. Yet in that short distance sounds must travel through air, membrane, bone and liquid. Even then the journey is not over. The sounds must be changed into nerve impulses and carried along nerve fibers to your brain, so that you can recognize and understand the meaning of the sounds.

The "ears" on the sides of your head act simply as

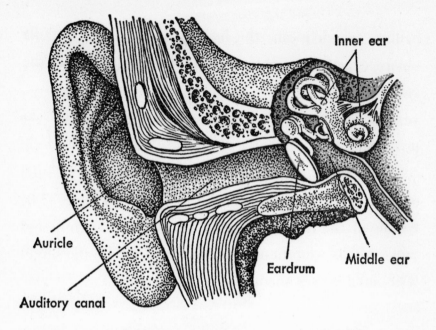

Inner ear

Auricle

Auditory canal

Eardrum

Middle ear

In your ear sounds travel through air, membrane, bone and liquid.

funnels to collect the vibrations of sound. Doctors call them the auricles.

Inside each auricle is an opening and a short passage called the auditory canal. The auricle and the auditory canal are known as the outer ear.

The auditory canal reaches only about an inch inside the skull. It can go no farther because its way is barred by a thin flexible membrane. This membrane is your eardrum. When the vibrations of sound enter your outer ear, they reach the eardrum and cause it to vibrate.

On the other side of your eardrum there is a small cavity called the middle ear. Inside this are three very tiny bones. Each one has a special name which describes its shape. They are called the hammer, the anvil and the stirrup.

These three miniature bones are connected in such a way that they pass on the sounds you hear. The handle of the hammer is attached to your eardrum and picks up its vibrations, passing them on to the anvil. The anvil passes them on to the stirrup.

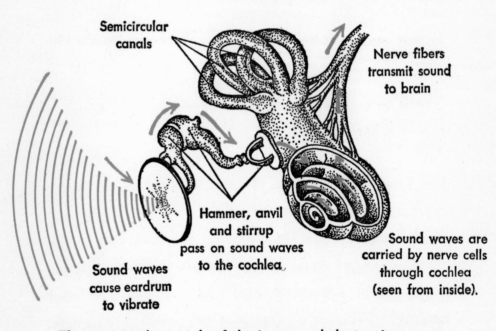

Semicircular canals

Nerve fibers transmit sound to brain

Hammer, anvil and stirrup pass on sound waves to the cochlea.

Sound waves cause eardrum to vibrate

Sound waves are carried by nerve cells through cochlea (seen from inside).

The semicircular canals of the inner ear help to give you a sense of balance.

The stirrup fits into a small opening leading to the inner ear. When the stirrup vibrates, the sounds pass on through a fluid called the perilymph, and then into a most beautiful and complicated spiral passage carved in the bone. This is called the cochlea, which means like the shell of a snail. With the cochlea are the special nerve cells of your sense of hearing. Finally, these pass on the messages to nerve fibers which go to the center of hearing in your brain.

In the inner ear is another organ, which gives you your sense of balance. It consists of three small semi-circular canals and two little sacs, filled with fluid. The slightest movement of your head causes the fluid in the canals to move, affecting nerve endings. These pass the information on to your brain so that it can adjust your muscles to balance yourself.

Your Eyes and How They Work

If you have ever taken photographs with a good camera, you will find it easy to understand how your eyes do their work of seeing. The eye is like a camera, except that it adapts itself for any kind of picture.

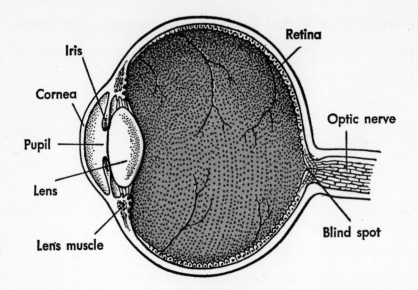

A cross section of the eye (greatly enlarged) shows the relation of the cornea, pupil and lens.

Also it goes on taking pictures as long as your eyes are open.

The eye is almost perfectly round, with a slight bulge in front. It changes only a little in size as you grow. In a newborn baby the eye is about three-quarters of an inch across. In adults it is about an inch. This explains why babies seem to have such beautiful big eyes. The rest of the face grows quite a lot, but the eye grows hardly at all.

The outside of the eye is very strong and firm. It is white, except where it bulges in front, and here it is transparent so that light can pass through. The transparent bulge is called the cornea. Its main purpose is to protect the eye from damage.

Behind the cornea is a thin delicate disc called the iris. The eye gets its color from the iris, which may be blue, gray, brown or hazel. The other side of the iris is deep purple.

In the center of the iris there is a circular hole called

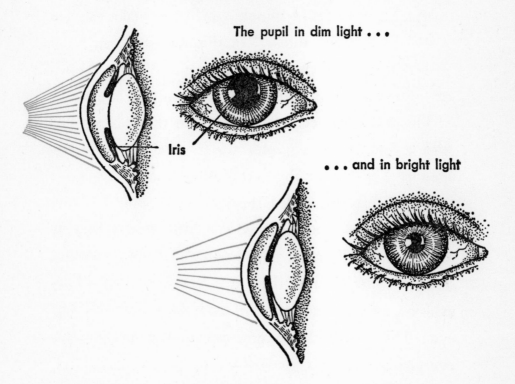

The pupil in dim light . . .

Iris

. . . and in bright light

In dim light the pupil becomes larger to permit more light to pass through. In bright light it is much smaller.

the pupil. The size of this hole is controlled by two sets of muscles. In dim light, the muscles cause the hole to become larger to allow more light to pass through. In bright light the size of the pupil is reduced to prevent the strong light from hurting the eye.

Immediately behind the pupil is the lens of the eye, a tiny transparent disc only about one-third of an inch in diameter, thin at the edges and thick in the middle. Around it is a ring of muscle which can make the lens a little smaller and thicker. In this way you can focus objects sharply when they are close to your eye. When the muscle is relaxed, you can see sharply at a distance.

The space between the cornea and the lens is filled with a liquid that is mostly water, called the aqueous humor. The rest of the eye is filled with a soft clear jelly-like material, called the vitreous humor.

The lens of the eye forms a picture of whatever you are looking at, like the lens of a camera, and this picture is projected on the back of the eye. Here there is a thin membrane called the retina, containing the nerve endings which are sensitive to light. These nerve endings are of two kinds. One is shaped like a rod, the other like a cone. The rods are more sensitive in dim light. The cones, scientists believe, enable us to see colors. From the rods and cones, the picture you see passes along nerve fibers to your brain.

At the back of the eye there is one small spot where you cannot see at all. This is the point where the optic nerve, carrying all the nerve fibers of the retina, enters the eye. It is known as the blind spot. You can test your own blind spot by looking at this illustration:

Close your left eye, or put your hand over it, and hold this page up so that the bird is in front of your right eye. Look as steadily as you can at the bird. You will still be able to see the black cat. Now, move the book away from you slowly, and you will find that the black cat suddenly disappears. The reason is that its image has fallen on your blind spot. If you move the page a fraction of an inch farther, the black cat will reappear. Of course, your eye makes allowances for the blind spot, and it does not interfere with your normal sight at all.

How Life
Goes On

All the cells in the body come from two special cells. These are called the ovum, or egg cell, and the sperm cell.

Your own life started from the meeting of these two cells. One, the ovum, was provided by your mother. The other, the sperm, was provided by your father. Your father and mother started their lives in the same way, and so did their fathers and mothers, and so did each of your ancestors, all the way back to the first human beings from whom we are all descended. These two mysterious living cells, ovum and sperm, are the links in the long chain of life, binding the countless generations together.

There is a great advantage in having life start from two cells. In this way, a child inherits characteristics

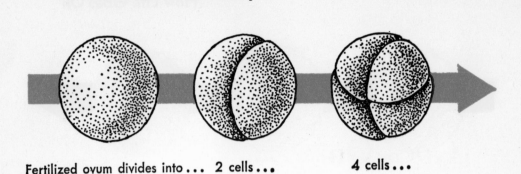

Fertilized ovum divides into ... 2 cells ...   4 cells ...

from both its father and mother. If life started only from an ovum, a child could only inherit the characteristics of its mother. The two-cell, or sexual, method of reproduction results in a greater variety of human beings and animals.

The nucleus of a complete human cell contains 48 particles called chromosomes. But the nucleus of the ovum contains only 24 chromosomes, and the same is true of the sperm. Only when the ovum and the sperm combine do we get the full number of 48. When this happens, the ovum is said to be fertilized.

Then it can begin the process of multiplying. It divides, making two complete cells; these divide, making four complete cells; and so the process goes on. It is hard to believe, but to make the thirty thousand million million cells that compose the whole of the human body, the cells divide only about fifty times.

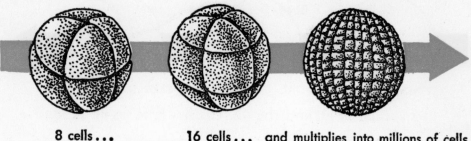

8 cells...   16 cells... and multiplies into millions of cells

The ovum is the largest cell produced by the human body. It can just be seen by the human eye. If you looked at it under a microscope, you would see that it is almost perfectly round.

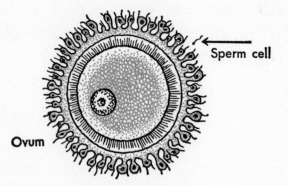

Sperm cell

Ovum

The sperm cell is tiny compared to the ovum. Without a microscope you could not see it. Its shape is different in every way. It has a small head, flattened and rather pointed at the top, and a long thin tail, ten

Sperm

times longer than the head. The sperm normally lives in a special fluid, and the tail enables it to swim around very vigorously. For its size, a sperm can swim quite fast—as much as four to six inches an hour.

When a baby girl is born, she already has in her body about four hundred thousand special cells which can become egg cells. We do not know whether any more are formed later; most scientists believe not.

Since only one egg cell and one sperm cell are necessary to start a new life, why are there so many egg cells? We can only guess that it is a way of making absolutely sure that the chain of life will go on.

In the early years of a girl's life, the egg cells are dormant, or asleep. They are also immature, which means that they are not yet ready to play their part in creating new life. They lie in two organs called ovaries, each about the size and shape of an almond. There is one on each side of the body, in the upper part of the pelvis.

In the gradual process of growing up, however, changes begin to appear which show that the girl is becoming a woman. And one of the most remarkable things is that the first egg cell escapes from an ovary and starts a journey through her body.

Close to each ovary there is a narrow tube, about four inches long, with an open end which looks like a fringe of petals. These tubes are called the Fallopian tubes.

As the egg cell leaves the ovary, it is caught in the fringed open end of the Fallopian tube near by. Very slowly, it passes through the Fallopian tube, a journey that takes about four days.

Each immature egg cell in the ovaries has 48 chromosomes. But an egg cell can have only 24 chromosomes if

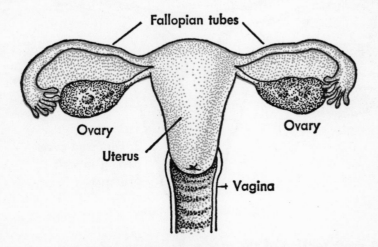

The female reproductive organs

it is to combine with a sperm having 24 chromosomes. So, as the egg cell travels through the Fallopian tube, it divides. The large part contains the 24 necessary chromosomes. The other part, which is very tiny, contains the 24 unwanted chromosomes. The small part, breaks up and disappears. The large part is the mature egg cell.

The Fallopian tubes lead into the uterus, or womb. This is a hollow organ with thick muscular walls, about three inches long and shaped like a pear. It is

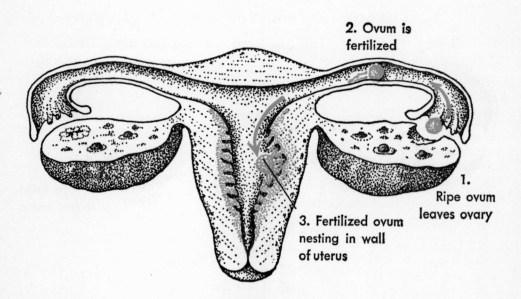

2. Ovum is fertilized

1. Ripe ovum leaves ovary

3. Fertilized ovum nesting in wall of uterus

A cross section of the uterus, Fallopian tubes and ovaries at the beginning of pregnancy

inside the uterus that a fertilized egg cell develops and is nourished for nine months as it grows into a baby.

Each time an egg cell leaves one of the ovaries, the uterus prepares to do its important work. The lining of the uterus becomes thicker and softer to receive the fertilized egg cell, and its blood vessels are filled with more blood than usual to provide nourishment.

But when an unfertilized egg cell passes from the Fallopian tubes into the uterus, there is no need for these preparations. Since an unfertilized egg cell can-

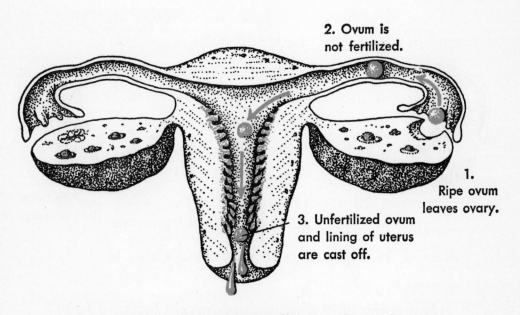

2. Ovum is
not fertilized.

1.
Ripe ovum
leaves ovary.

3. Unfertilized ovum
and lining of uterus
are cast off.

A cross section of the uterus, Fallopian tubes and ovaries during menstruation

not develop into a baby, the soft lining of the uterus and the extra blood are not required. So the body simply casts them off. They leave the uterus through the vagina, or birth canal, the passage through which babies come into the world.

As a girl grows a little older, this takes place every twenty-eight days or so. Usually it lasts three to five days. Doctors call it the menstrual period, or menstruation, from the Latin word meaning monthly.

The male sperm cells are produced even more lavishly than egg cells. In the course of a man's lifetime his body will produce hundreds of billions of sperms—enough to populate the world many times over.

Like the egg cells in the ovaries, sperm cells are formed in two small organs called the testes. But, unlike the ovaries, the testes are close together and lie outside the body, in a sac called the scrotum. Outside the body, too, is the organ known as the penis.

Between the ages of twelve to sixteen, a boy begins to show signs that he is becoming a man. His voice deepens; hair sprouts on his chin and chest; his body grows big and strong.

This is the time when the sperm cells begin to form in larger and larger numbers in the two testes. But

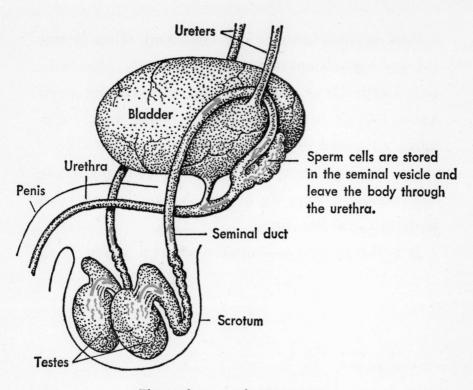

Ureters

Bladder

Sperm cells are stored
in the seminal vesicle and
leave the body through
the urethra.

Urethra

Penis

Seminal duct

Scrotum

Testes

The male reproductive organs

instead of leaving the body one by one, like egg cells,
the sperms are stored away. From each of the testes
a tube goes up into the pelvis and curves around to
join a narrow canal which runs through the penis.
The name of this canal is the urethra. The sperm cells,
swimming in a fluid called the seminal fluid, collect
in the two seminal ducts and in small pouches called
the seminal vesicles. Here they remain until they leave
the body through the urethra.

And so the chain of life is continued, using as links the tiny egg cell and much tinier sperm cell. How these cells carry life we do not know, and we may never know. All we really know so far is that 24 chromosomes are added to 24 chromosomes; tiny particles of chemicals combine; and in some completely mysterious and marvelous way life begins. A new human being starts to come into being.

It is the greatest and most wonderful secret of all.

Index

Index

Index

About the author of this book:

BERNARD GLEMSER was born in England, but has lived in the United States for more than twelve years and is now an American citizen.

In preparing a book on the work of one of the leading medical research centers in this country, Mr. Glemser began intensive reading about medicine and physiology and discovered himself completely fascinated with the wonders of the human body. It was as a result of this study that this Allabout Book came into being.

Mr. Glemser has written many adult novels including *Gallery of Women* and *The Lieutenant*. He is also the author of a successful book for boys, *Radar Commandos*.

About the illustrator of this book:

FELIX TRAUGOTT is one of the nation's foremost medical illustrators. Since 1936 he has been director of the medical art and photography department of the Jersey City Medical Center, and he also has taught a special class of medical scholars from Harvard University.

Mr. Traugott has done the illustrating for the Scott, Foresman Health and Personal Development Series; the American Book Company Health Series and is currently working on the Macmillan Science Life Series. He has also illustrated many biology books for high school and college, and professional books on surgery and medicine.

allabout books